MIES VAN DER ROHE
BARCELONA PAVILION

Ignasi de Solà-Morales

Cristian Cirici

Fernando Ramos

GG®

Editorial Gustavo Gili, S.A.

08029 Barcelona   Rosselló, 87-89
Spain
Tel. (343) 322 81 61   Fax (343) 322 92 05

Graphic design: Eulàlia Coma

Translation: Graham Thomson

© Editorial Gustavo Gili, S.A., Barcelona, 1993

ISBN: 84-252-1607-9
Printed in Singapore

Summary

Introduction

It might be said that this book on the German Pavilion designed by Mies van der Rohe for the Barcelona International Exposition, which we have recently reconstructed, amounts to little more than the design report of our project.

We are conscious of having enjoyed a unique experience. As architects, we undertook the reconstruction of one of the paradigm buildings of 20th century architecture. We set out from an assortment of differing backgrounds and experiences, and found ourselves faced with the singular circumstance of a task of reconstruction for which there was an abundance of information relating to what we were to rebuild, yet not enough to establish, beyond all doubt, the characteristics belonging to Mies's mythic building.

Our work, our undertaking, was a project. An atypical project, however, in as much as the relationship between investigative study, critical decisions and technical solutions was different from what would be the norm in a conventional architectural project.

This present volume consists of two fundamental parts: in the first place, a resumé of such information as we were able to assemble with respect to the 1929 building and its critical interpretation. Secondly, an explanation of the specific technical solution which constituted our response to the problem confronting us. The explanation of this process, then, is the principle purpose of this book. However, this explanation also has an informative dimension, which in our view serves to complete it and add to its interest. For this reason, the book also attempts to offer a full description of the information and the documents at our disposal in relation to the 1929 building, as well as to the reconstructed building. To these two bodies of material we have also added an extensive bibliography dealing with the Pavilion throughout the course of its fifty years of physical existence: at first only virtual; then, as it is now, finally reconstructed.

We also wish to note that the present book was in fact prepared between 1985 and 1988, and that a number of unforeseen difficulties subsequently delayed its publication. For this reason, it has not always been possible to include in full all the material which has come to light during the last few years.

This book has been made possible thanks to the indispensable contributions of a series of individuals and institutions, to all of whom we wish to express our gratitude. First of all, to those presently in charge of the Fundació Mies van der Rohe in Barcelona for their generosity in putting their documentation and resources at our disposal. We are also indebted to the Museum of Modern Art and to the Mies van der Rohe Archive in New York, and to the Preussischer Kulturbesitz in Berlin, for the invaluable documentary material they made available to us. Our thanks, too, to Joaquim Romaguera and Xavier Güell, who guided the book thorugh publication with the utmost professionalism; and to Isabel Bachs and Ton Salvadó, whose involvement at every stage of the book's preparation was as intelligent as it was unstintingly dedicated to attaining the goal we set ourselves.

Ignasi de Solà-Morales/Cristian Cirici/
Fernando Ramos
Barcelona, August 1992

I. The German Pavilion in Barcelona. The 1929 building

1. Werner Blaser: *Mies van der Rohe: the art of the structure* (trilingual), Carlos Hirsch Editor, Buenos Aires, 1965.

2. Dr. Sergius Ruegenberg, who worked with Mies van der Rohe during his European period, contributed to the design and construction of the Barcelona project. After the Second World War he produced a number of drawings, presenting his own version of the Pavilion in general plans, technical details and perspectives which were never widely published, due to Ruegenberg's desire to retain control of them with a view to their possible use in concrete projects. The relationship between the two men is recounted in his article, «Ludwig Mies van der Rohe: 1886-1969», in *Deutsche Bauzeitung*, September 1st, 1969. Dr. Ruegenberg's drawings and perspectives have recently started to be published, at times combined or confused with Mies' own drawings. See: Sandra Honey: «Who and What Inspired Mies van der Rohe in Germany», *Architectural Design*, n.º 3-4, 1979; Mario Ciammitti/Giuseppe Di Giovine: «Per conoscere il Padiglione di Mies», in *Parametro*, n.º 122, December 1983, and also «Mies van der Rohe. European Works», in *Architectural Monographs*, London, 1986.

3. The arduous task of cataloguing over 20,000 documents carried out by Ludwig Glaeser between 1968 and 1980, when he was in charge of the Mies van der Rohe Archive, forms the basis of our current level of understanding. Prof. Glaeser whose extensive study of the Pavilion is to be published soon, has already made his considerable knowledge of the subject available in his book *Furniture and Furniture Drawings from the Design Collection at the Mies van der Rohe Archive,* New York, 1977, and in the exhibition catalogue *Ludwig Mies van der Rohe. The Barcelona Pavilion*, Washington, D.C., 1979.

1. The state of research

During many years, the execution and the characteristics of the German Pavilion for the Barcelona Universal Exposition of 1929 were entirely unknown. In spite of the growing recognition accorded to the building in the years after the Second World War, the swiftness of its disappearance after the event for which it was built seems to have contributed to the many uncertainties and imprecisions which it seemed that no one was in any position to clarify. The documentation was far from accessible, the Civil War in Spain and the Second World War in Germany having so dramatically affected many of the individuals and institutions who had been responsible for the production and administration of that piece of work recognized as fundamental for the architecture of the 20th century.

For the above reasons, there could be no detailed and in-depth understanding of the characteristics of the German Pavilion until relatively recently. The attempt to recreate through drawings and plans the most exact definition of the building did not come about until Werner Blaser, then working on a monograph study of Mies van der Rohe, produced a number of new drawings of the European projects in collaboration with Mies himself and his studio in Chicago.[1] In the case of the German Pa-

vilion, it is now possible to recognize the importance of Blaser's work, even admitting the limitations to be ascribed to Mies' testimony thirty years after the fact in drawings which, while they afford previously unknown insights, tend not to reproduce with complete fidelity the reality of the building constructed in 1929.

The second attempt at redrawing the project was undertaken by Dr Ruegenberg, who devoted years to preparing what he considered to be the most reliable documentary evidence available for a minutely detailed description of the building and the clarification of all its dimensional and technical characteristics.[2] Looking beyond the restrictions imposed by Dr Ruegenberg on the dissemination of his documents —documents which, when they have been made public, have thrown much light on a considerable number of questions of detail and technical execution— these amount to what is more properly a personal proposal of a new way of constructing the building than a faithful description of the material characteristics of the building as actually constructed in Barcelona in 1929.

For this reason we can say that it is only fairly recently, with the architect Ludwig Glaeser as director of the Mies van der Rohe Archive, working alongside the historian Wolf Tegethoff under the guid-

ance of Arthur Drexler from the Architecture and Design Section of the Museum of Modern Art in New York, that any substantial advance has been made in our detailed knowledge of the building's characteristics and the modifications imposed on it during the course of its progressive definition.[3] The exhibition on the German Pavilion organized by Ludwig Glaeser for the MOMA in 1979 and subsequently shown throughout the United States and Europe, and specifically in Barcelona, represented a first attempt at compiling the information of all kinds —graphic, written, and direct testimony— painstakingly collected by the MOMA researchers. Wolf Tegethoff's doctoral thesis, initially published in the catalogue for an exhibition in Krefeld and later issued in book form in Germany and North America, subsequently provided further illumination of the set of problems presented by the 1929 Pavilion.

However, it was only at the start of the eighties, with the imminent celebration of the centenary of Mies van der Rohe's birth, that the inventory of sources —Berlin, Barcelona, Chicago, etc.— and the comparative study of the collected data resulted in a more precise understanding of what the building had been, of the vicissitudes affecting its architectural definition and its critical fortunes, in a way that had not been achieved in the past.

The efforts of those of us who worked on the reconstruction in Barcelona, which was inaugurated in 1986, but whose origins go back precisely to those first years of the eighties, are absolutely indebted to the scientific and historiographic labours of those who went before us, and in particular to those architects and historians we have mentioned above.

The text and the graphic materials presented below, constituting a resumé of the body of information now at our disposal, is to a certain extent a synthesis

Fig. 1. Panoramic view of the Avinguda M.ª Cristina, from a period poster.

of the work of information which we ourselves were obliged to undertake in order properly to carry out our task of construction; it is also, however, to a great extent a summary of the most solidly researched comparative information available to date in published form.

2. The architect and the place

The Barcelona International Exposition, inaugurated by King Alfonso XIII on the 19th of May, 1929, was the consummation of a project long cherished by the city and repeatedly delayed for reasons of one kind or another. Barcelona had hosted the Universal Exposition of 1888, and although this had been an event of more limited scope the positive contributions it had brought to the city soon gave rise to a desire to host a second and grander exhibition, more daring, thematically more incisive and urbanistically more ambitious in its implications for the city. From the beginning of the new century the idea of another International Exposition was put forward on a number of occassions, but it was not until 1914 that a committee of industrialists and politicians finally took the initiative of announcing the new exhibition.[5] With the decisive support of the City Council of Barcelona, the organizing committee of the International Exposition of Electrical Industries set in motion the process necessary for the celebration three years from then, in 1917, of this latest international event. The outbreak of the Great War in Europe a few months later put a halt to the project, which was postponed, on the ending of the war in 1918, until 1923. These were not idle years, however. Within a few months of the setting up of the Management Committee, the architect Josep Puig i Cadafalch presented a sketch design scheme for the Exposition site which, in its second phase, was developed as three separate projects: by the architects Lluís Domènech

i Montaner and Manuel Vega i March, by Enrique Sagnier and Augusto Font, and, in the third of the zones into which the complex was divided, by Puig i Cadafalch himself.

The conception of the Exposition as it was developed in the scheme by Puig i Cadafalch and his fellow architects followed the accepted criteria of use for International Exhibitions at that time, based on a system of grand palaces laid out around some coordinating element, which was in this case to be the great avenue ascending from the Plaza de España to culminate on the crest of the Montjuïc hill in the dominating mass of the Palau Nacional building.

From the 1870s on, this system had effectively taken the place of the primitive type of exposition design with its single great building in whose interior all the activites and exhibits were laid out either on the basis of means of production or of country. The system adopted in Barcelona consisted of a series of independent buildings devoted to different branches of production —Steelmaking, Transport, Textiles, Agriculture, Graphic Arts, Electricity, etc.— and subdivided internally into areas occupied by the industries of the different exhibiting nations. It is worth noting this approach to the organization of an exhibition —which was in due course, in the fifties, replaced by the concept of individual National Pavilions— in that an awareness of this circumstance helps us to understand the low level of integration of the national pavilions in the Barcelona Exposition of 1929.

In effect, the decision to establish national representation was formulated when the built structure was already basically in existence, and in line with the thematic criteria described above. For this reason, the organizers of the Barcelona Exposition, once it was decided in 1927 to propose that the presence of the various countries interested in taking part should consist not only of the exhibition of their products but of individual national pavilions, had to over-

come both the inertia of an established procedure that was already being implemented and the difficulty of an unforeseen architectonic intervention which proved anomalous and conflictive in relation to the general layout worked out by Puig i Cadafalch ten years earlier.

Fig. 2. Aerial view of the central zone of the Exposition with the German Pavilion on the right.

In the case of the German presence, the initial response was negative, with the protocols preparatory to the Exposition including reports from the German Embassy in Madrid and the Deutsches Ausstellungs und Messe Amt discounting the idea of a separate building representing Germany in addition to the specific displays for each branch of German manufacturing output.[6]

In fact, the nature of German participation was not formally decided until the middle of 1928. The agreement between the Spanish and German authorities is dated May 29th, 1928; that is, less than a year before the day of

4. Wolf Tegethoff: *Mies van der Rohe. Die Villen und Landhausprojekte,* Essen, 1981.

5. For a study of the Barcelona International Exposition of 1929 in its entirety, see Ignasi de Solà-Morales: *L'Exposició Internacional de Barcelona 1914-1929. Arquitectura i Ciutat,* Barcelona, 1985.

6. In a confidential report sent by the German ambassador in Madrid to the president of the Executive Committee of the Barcelona International Exposition, as late as September 13th, 1928 there was insistence that «it has been determined to discount as hardly practical the idea of constructing a German Pavilion», adding that «the fact that other nations should meanwhile have decided to construct pavilions of their own does not seem apt to motivate a change in the above decision, if for no other reason than that the short period of eight months still remaining would be insufficient to erect a building worthy of standing alongside the splendid Spanish palaces». Documentary Section, Files of the International Exposition, Institut Municipal d'Història, Barcelona, 1929.

7.   «Official communication Ministry Foreign Affairs notifying German Government accepts with pleasure invitation Spanish Government to participate Barcelona Exposition, having appointed Dr Georg von Schnitzler general commissioner», May 29th, 1928. Text of the telegram preserved in the archives of the organizing Delegation of the International Exposition of 1929. In a telegram dated May 30th, it was announced that the architect Mies van der Rohe would arrive in Barcelona «next Friday» (June 7th). Documentary Section, Files of the International Exposition, Institut Municipal d'Història, Barcelona, 1929.

8.   See W. Tegethoff, op. cit., n.º 4, pp. 73-74 and notes 21, 23 and 25.

9.   Walter Genzmer: «Der Deutsche Reichspavillon auf der Internationalen Ausstellung Barcelona», in Die Baugilde, n.º 1, 1929, pp. 1654-1657.

opening.[7] The decision to give the architect Mies van der Rohe the responsibility for the setting up of the physical fabric of the German Exposition buildings was made at the same time as the appointment of Dr Georg von Schnitzler as general commissioner, and those of Drs Kraemer, Herle and Matthies as assistant commissioners. Germany's participation was by then firmly agreed but imprecise, and certainly far from definite as regards the construction of a separate national pavilion.

The brief given to Mies van der Rohe, who immediately set out for Barcelona, where he arrived on June 7th, to make personal contact with the Exposition authorities, had reference to the series of spaces on which the various pavilions were to be constructed.

It seems that the first idea was to erect, alongside the different exhibition stands, a «lighthouse-tower» which would act as a signal beacon giving visual representation to the German presence. On this first lightning visit, as also on the second, on September 19th, in the company of Lilly Reich and Dr Schnitzler and his wife, Mies van der Rohe was fundamentally concerned with the fitting out of the stands in the different pavilions, asking for the technical specifications of the available spaces and negotiating in Barcelona with the Exposition architects to obtain the most suitable locations in each of the pavilions for the display of German produce.

In a report dating from this time the German authorities continue to insist that they have no intention of constructing a separate national pavilion in addition to the various stands.

We have no precise information to enable us to give a definite date for the change in policy, but Tegethoff suggests in his book that immediately following Mies' return from this second visit to Barcelona his Berlin office began the period of intense activity that was to continue uninterrupted until the opening ceremony.[8]

The article published by Walter Genzmer in Der Baugilde in 1929, which is one of our most valuable sources of firsthand information, refers to the matter of a change of site for the pavilion, with the German authorities apparently now being interested in the possibility of its construction. A Raumsraëpresentation, that is, a space freed of any practical use for exhibition and intended purely for official functions, was what Mies van der Rohe had to produce in the short time available from the end of September, 1928, to the date of the inauguration on the 26th of May of the following year.[9]

The Spanish authorities' response to the challenge of including separate national pavilions betrayed a tremendous poverty of architectonic ideas. Anyone unaware of the relationship between politics and architecture would be astonished to observe the attempts to introduce, without any kind of rational criterion, a considerable number of small buildings —the Italian, French, Danish,

Swedish, Yugoslav, Belgian and other pavilions— into a composition of such a markedly academic character, organized around a series of grand palaces, all designed by local architects. All of these pavilions were designed by architects from the respective countries, who set about the task with total disregard for the setting in which their work was to be constructed. The only one to dissociate himself from this poor, anomalous approach, perhaps best understood in terms of the conflicts surrounding the figure of Puig i Cadafalch after the Spanish coup d'état of 1923, was Mies van der Rohe.

Thus the architect commissioned by the German authorities to construct the fabric of their national presence made frequent trips to Barcelona; rejected the unthinkable site —dependent on the Pavilion of France, down at the bottom of the flight of steps leading up to the Palau Nacional— proffered by the Exposition's bureaucrats and proposed an alternative location in its stead. He contrived to move his pavilion from this excessively formalized, proportionally disadvantageous setting to win a place for the German Pavilion on the south rim of the Gran Plaza de la Fuente Mágica, the true heart of the exposition, behind eight tall sandstone Ionic columns erected by Puig i Cadafalch in 1923 to mark out the geometrical boundary of the great central area of the Exposition.

Fig. 3.   Aerial view with the German Pavilion on the left.

The chosen plot consisted of an elongated rectangle with a pronounced slope to the south, formed by the side of the hill climbing up towards the popular amusements of the Pueblo Español. To the east, the gigantic blind wall of the Palau de Victòria Eugenia would provide that element of contrast celebrated by the more intelligent critics of the day when they came to compare the geometry, the colour, the texture and the language of Mies' building with the traditional aspect of the architecture of the palace constructed by Puig i Cadafalch in 1923.

The position of this plot was by no means neutral. Not only did it have the blind wall of the Palau de Victòria Eugenia and the Ionic columns marking the boundary of the Gran Plaza, but its sloping form included one of the areas of richest vegetation in the gardens of Montjuïc, as well as the pedestrian route defined by the steps which, prior to construction of the German Pavilion, had constituted one of the points of connection between the esplanade and the Pueblo Español.

Faced with the offer of the first, trivial site, Mies' response was to request an alternative location, apparently marginal, but rich in territorial possibilities which the future building was to make its own, interiorizing them in the organization of the Pavilion as one of the most effective means of allowing a small, conventional representative space to root itself in its setting and emphasize the territorial conditions in which it also shared.

3. The evolution of the project

One thing that has been a constant problem in recreating the scheme for the German Pavilion in Barcelona is precisely its nonexistence. With the knowledge we now have at our disposal, we can say that this lack of a project as such should not be thought of as meaning that the original documents have been lost, but rather that, in our opinion, the process of designing and building the Pavilion was subject to so much pressure, haste and last-minute change that it would be misleading to speak of any definitive state, whether

as a drawing on paper showing how the building was intended to be, or even for the finished building, in the sense of its definitive physical materialization. The provisional nature of the building, to which we shall return in due course, is revealed, we believe, more in the open, changing character of many of the solutions and details embodied in it than in its lack of durability or in the fragility of its construction processes. In our judgement, the only thing that we can undertake to do at this stage, on the basis of the abundant but widely dispersed existing documents, is to recreate something of the process by which the solution ultimately adopted and constructed was given a physical form and a precise definition.

Wolf Tegethoff has painstakingly compared the various different pieces of information which make it possible to accurately recompose the process by which the building was defined, from the framing of the first ideas late in 1928 to the point where Mies' design team moved to Barcelona at the end of February, 1929.

According to verbal testimony recorded by Sergius Ruegenberg[10], the earliest work on the project was centred on a model assembled from movable pieces, used to experiment with the range of variable positions for the different planes of the elements of partition and closure. For some of these positions tested on the model, Mies himself had already determined the most interesting solutions by means of perspective sketches which revealed repeated effects of transparency or interrelation.[11] The presence of vertical planes sliding between the flat surface of the Pavilion's roof and the cubic mass of the podium is evident from the start, as is the cutting effect produced by the main flight of steps, positioned from the very outset perpendicular to the main access of the Plaza. Initially this stairway seems to have been conceived as excavated, carved out of the mass of the podium, and only later more clearly defined as a point of articulation of two parallel sliding planes which were to constitute the side of the podium facing towards the Gran Plaza de la Fuente Mágica.

10. See W. Tegethoff, *op. cit.*, p. 75.

11. The majority of these perspectives, along with others drawn by Dr Ruegenberg, are now to be found in the Kunstbibliotheck of the Staatlichte Museen of the Preussischer Kulturbesitz.

Fig. 4. Preliminary sketch (pencil on paper).

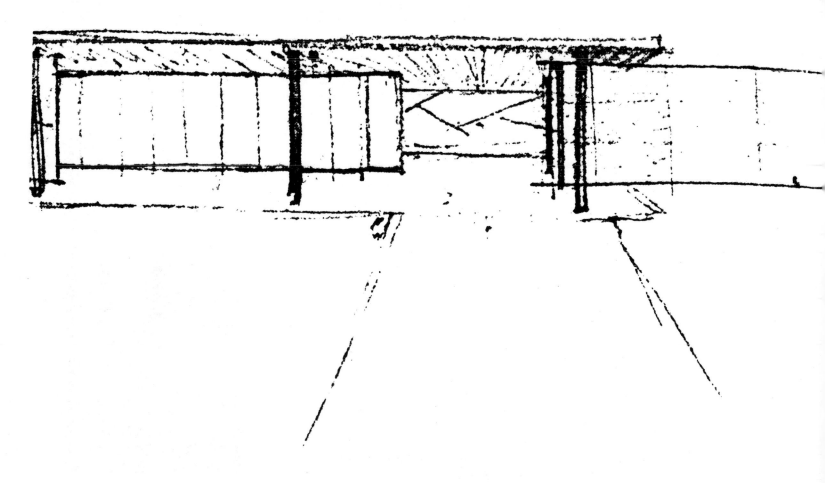

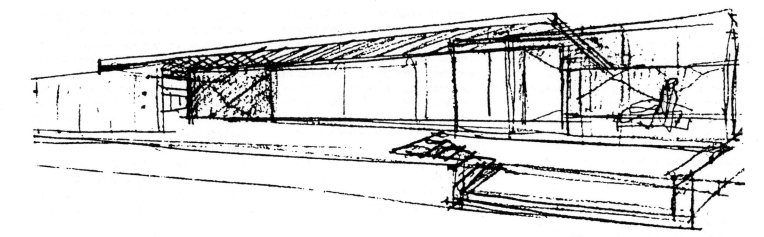

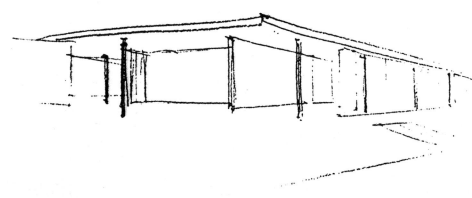

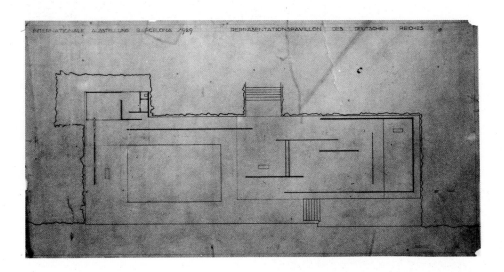

Fig. 7. First preliminary drawing (1928) (pencil on transparent paper).

In these early treatments of the project, the idea of the structure seems not to be clearly defined. The presence of a number of steel pillars, represented on the model by lengths of wire, as indicated in the notes in the margin of one of the drawings, tends to suggest the idea of an autonomous load-bearing structure. This idea is further supported by the drawings reproduced in figures 4 and 5, the first of which shows the rear of the Pavilion with the definition of the entrance from the steps leading to the Pueblo Español, while the second, possibly with three rows of pillars, shows the more definitive position of the wall of «Alpine green» marble and the transparent glazed wall adjacent to the access stairway. It is possible that these drawings in fact correspond to a later phase of the project's evolution, given that they present solutions that are much closer to the definitive ones than those to be seen in the drawing in figure 6. In these, there are no structural elements: the roof is evidently supported on the edge of the vertical walls, the main flight of steps presents the idea of a void excised out of the prismatic mass of the podium, while of the two areas with ornamental pools, one appears to be visually open to the stairway space, with the other, by contrast, closed off by a travertine wall of vertically arranged slabs that is still far removed from the definitive solution.

All of this series of drawings which can be related to the working model mentioned above seems to be summarized, within the oscillations of criteria which are still apparent in this trial-and-error stage, in the plan shown in figure 7, conserved in the MOMA's archives; this plan, drawn at a scale of 1/100, represents a fairly precise attempt at defining the dimensions of the project. What makes the experimental situation of the project at this point in time all the more evident is the clarity of certain aspects in contrast to the major modificacions which were still to be introduced.

The disposition of the walls and the outer fabric in the roof and the forms of the smaller pool and the main stairway are by now almost definitive. The opening of the larger pool and its proportions, the form of the office volume, the sides of the podium and the characteristics of the load-bearing structure are still, in this drawing, somewhat problematic. We find here the idea of the three podiums for sculptures: one in either pool, plus a third opposite the rear facade of the tinted glass box which acts as a light well serving the interior of the Pavilion. The carpentry detailing is a long way here from its final form, and the building's relationship with its surroundings is not that finally arrived at.

In the correspondence on file in the MOMA archives there are numerous references to the changes which had to be made in the exact siting of the building in relation to the Palau de Victòria Eugenia, to the existing flight of steps leading up to the Pueblo Español and to the parallel street which passed in front of the Pavilion between the travertine wall and the row of Ionic columns, mentioned above, enclosing the area of the Gran Plaza.[12]

When, some time in February 1929, work on the project was suspended for several weeks for economic reasons[13], it seems that the exorbitant rise in costs was due, amongst other causes, to the unforeseen uprooting and resurfacing of the road attendant on the definitive decision as to the exact site of the building. Moving it closer to the Palau de Victòria Eugenia, as well as towards the centre of the Gran Plaza, evidently in the interests of the scheme, added to the cost of the work and modified the character of the side facades and the rear of the building, as can be seen in the subsequent drawings.

A second study in the elaboration of the plan is conserved in the Mies van der Rohe Archive, reproduced here in figure 8. In this plan, the general dimensions of the building have changed, having been appreciably reduced to their definitive values. At the same time, this plan presents the broken treatment of the podium which Mies was to retain from this moment on, as it appeared in the built work. The earlier conception of the podium as an autonomous platform raised off the floor has given way to a prismatic element, its composition fractured by the opening of the main stairway and sharply interrupted as it turns on the two side facades, forming a cutaway figure which gives way to the smooth, flush-set surface of the enclosing walls which emerge directly from the floor. The podium does not return at the rear, so that the horizontal plane of the floor of the Pavilion tends to favour a gentle encounter with the ascending slope of the hillside, going on to find the level of the existing flight of steps in the Montjuïc gardens.

Alongside this definition of the fragmentary character of the podium, we find on this ground plan the independent load-bearing structure, which at this stage of its evolution consists of six cruciform pillars supporting the greater part of the roof surface, while perhaps leaving the side walls with the task of supporting the area closest to the small pool. It is only in a more advanced study (fig. 9) that we are introduced to the definitive structure of eight pillars as it was actually constructed, within a few months of the drawing of this plan.

The plan we are concerned with here still features the three bases for statues, executed just as they were sketched in on some of the drawings now held in Berlin. The layout of the office building is different from what we saw in the previous plan, and we should note here that in later detail drawings which can be seen in New York there are a number of variants which help us to understand the continual changes to which the treatment of this part of the Pavilion was subjected; an aspect which, in our view, even in the completed version fails to present a solution that can plausibly be considered as definitive. At all events, the programme for the annexe building of two offices plus a toilet is one of the scheme's most variable elements, evolving from a more open treatment to the final version, enclosed, with high windows, as constructed. Of the series of details relating to this part of the building we have a set of three schematic elevations (fig. 12) which show us how the flexibility in the handing of these spaces was conceived without the limitations imposed by the excavation of the site out of the hillside, on the basis of an imaginary flat surface open on three sides. When, with construction about to commence, the limitations of the topography became apparent, the solution adopted was to make do with a greater spatial simplicity and a drastic reduction in the number of openings.

12. The minutes of the meeting addressing problems of increased construction costs and relating these changes in detail, dated July 8th, 1929, are in the Mies van der Rohe Archive, MOMA.

13. Regarding the interruption of the building work, Tegethoff provides a fundamental document taken from the minutes of the Werkbund meeting, at which Mies hilself, then vice-president, reported on the state of the project under construction. There are also a number of letters in the MOMA files which record this unforeseen change of attitude by the authorities which halted progress during several weeks. See W. Tegethoff, *op. cit.*, p. 74, and notes 24-25.

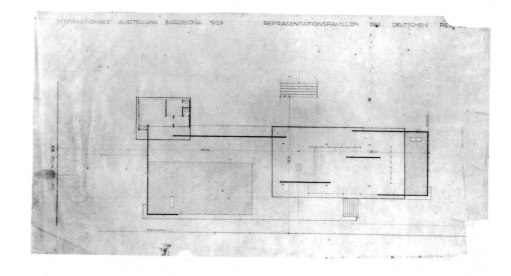

Fig. 8. Second preliminary drawing (1928) (pencil and coloured pencil on transparent paper).

Fig. 9. Definitive plan.

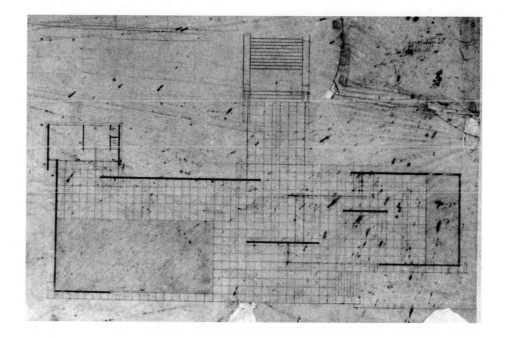

14. See I. de Solà-Morales, *op. cit.*, note 5, pp. 41 ff.

15. We would like to note here the numerous laudatory texts which appeared at the time of the Exposition and run counter to the opinion expressed by Juan Pablo Bonta that Mies van der Rohe's Pavilion initially provoked no interest. See J. P. Bonta: *Anatomía de la interpretación en arquitectura. Reseña semiótica de la crítica del Pabellón de Barcelona de Mies van der Rohe*, Barcelona, 1975. It is enough to refer to the Diario Oficial of the International Exposition, in which more than twenty different articles voiced favourable, positive opinions regarding the German Pavilion. See, too, the article by Marius Gifreda in *D'Ací i d'Allà*, for December 1929: «L'arquitectura de l'Exposició», pp. 89-93, and the views reflected in local newspapers such as *La Vanguardia, La Noche, La Publicitat, La Veu de Catalunya, El Noticiero Universal, La Nau, Las Noticias* and others.

In this plan, as in the previous one, there is still no sign of the bench of travertine stone in front of the wall of the same material. We do not know precisely when Mies decided to include this highly characteristic element, but it is clear that this must have occurred at an advanced stage of the scheme's definition. The MOMA archives have a working drawing (fig. 10) of the stone bench. Perhaps its most noteworthy feature is the extreme simplicity of its construction, the supports palpably cubic —although the dimensions of the three sides are not exactly equal— and the thick slab of the seat cut in such a way that it coincides neither with the sequence of the paving nor with that of the wall behind it: the absolute limits of this element are sufficiently autonomous to

detach it from both the start of the wall which serves it as backrest and the end of the pool which seems to mark its position (fig. 13).

In this bench we find confirmation of the freedom with which each material and each element establishes its own dimensionality, entirely avoiding any attempt at imposing a rigid, universal dimensional law to unify all the parts of the building by referring them to a single uniform module.

We can still discern in the plan we are considering here a different layout in the relationship between the existing flight of steps to the rear and the Pavilion's rear «entrance» or «exit».

On the one hand, we know that this stairway existed and formed part of a footpath that led up from the Plaza de la Fuente Mágica to the Pueblo Español; its construction most probably dates from the time when Rubió i Tudurí and Forestier were commissioned to landscape the part of Montjuïc above what was then the «Gran Vía K» —now the Avinguda de Rius i Taulet— sometime around 1916.[14] On the other hand, we can see how the various different drawings of the general plan, and the perspective sketches, show that the position of this flight of steps remains practically constant: always centred in relation to the rear access and occupying a frontal position. Nevertheless, we know that the dimensions of the building changed, becoming smaller, and that it shifted its position relative to the blind wall of the Palau de Victòria Eugenia. From this we can deduce that, throughout the project, the position of this stairway must have been taken as a fixed and immovable reference point, determining not only the exact siting of the building but even its dimensions.

Fig. 13. The travertine bench and wall during construction.

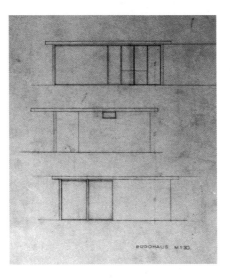

Fig. 12. Elevations of the annexes.

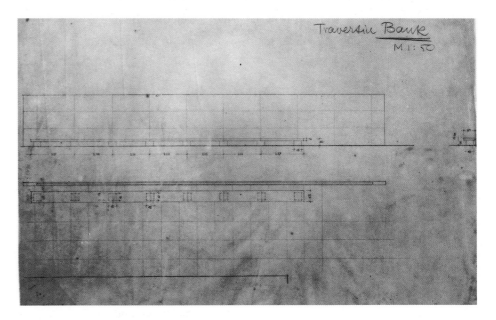

Fig. 10. Detail of the travertine bench.

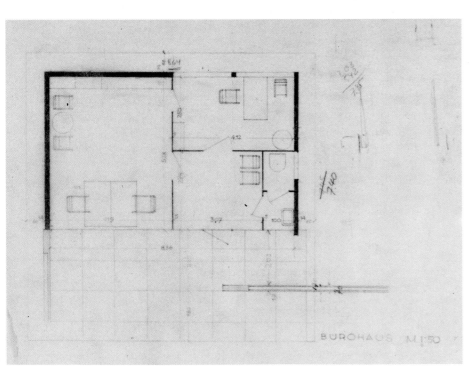

Fig. 11. Plan of the annexes.

The design solution adopted to produce the connection between the building and this stairway also varies through time, appearing as an extension of the stone paving of the podium, or, as it was finally fixed, by means of a rectangle of flattened sand at a level somewhat lower than that of the building's platform. The variations in this solution to be seen in the different ground plans, even in those drawn after the building's construction, demonstrate the conceptual difficulty of resolving the connection between a rectangular podium that gave the impression of being cut off at the sides but which, at precisely that point, was extended out to seek connection once again with an external element such as the existing flight of steps.

4. Materials and construction

It has been repeated *ad nauseam* that one of the reasons for the impact produced by the German Pavilion was the modernity of its materials. However, this widely accepted assertion needs more careful consideration, since it is by no means obvious that a building constructed basically of stone must, by virtue of its materials, be a modern, innovative construction. The journalists of the time spoke of the reflections, the highlights, the perfection and the advanced technology demonstrated by the materials of the German Pavilion.[15] In fact, we can now see that Mies van der Rohe's originality lay not so much in the radical newness of the materials on view, but in managing to make these express an ideal of modernity through the vigour of their geometry, the exactness of their cutting and shaping and the clarity of their assembly.

Even in the earliest drawings it seems that Mies van der Rohe had little doubt about the presence of water, glass and marble as the basic surfaces that would give the building its character. The article by Genzmer referred to above[16] gives the most precise and detailed information about the materials used. We can affirm that the building's base and its principal defining walls (fig. 14) are executed in slabs of Roman travertine provided by the Berlin company of Köstner und Gottschalk. Not only a beautiful working drawing bearing the name of the firm, but the advertisements placed in the International Exposition press attest to the fact that they supplied the stone for construction.

The paving was laid in square slabs measuring approximately 1.10×1.10 m, although the actual plan as it has come down to us reveals the extent to which the dimensions of this basic module were subject to multiple corrections which made it necessary to move the joints of the stone slabs a few millimetres in one direction or another to fit them to the previously determined position of the vertical walls and the pillars. Some people have concluded from this plan that in effect Mies gave himself free rein in modifying a grid that was never rigorously adopted.[17] We believe this not to have been the case, and impossible to deduce from a detailed scrutiny of the minute differences introduced more as fine adjustments than from any deliberate desire for variation on a hypothetical module.[18] In any case, it is just as true to affirm that for Mies in the Barcelona Pavilion there was, as we have said, no single module, and in fact there was a separate modular network for each of the materials used.

The travertine of the vertical walls had a double dimension of roughly 2.20×1.10 m, the walls being based on a double slab 3 cm thick with a load-bearing metal structure in its interior.

This was also the system used for the walls of green marble, of which there were two types in the Pavilion: one known in the twenties as green Tinos marble, obtained from quarries on the Greek mainland, and the green Alpine marble, supplied for the most part by the great stone quarries of the Valle d'Aosta. We should note that in the legend supplied by Genzmer to the plan published with his article on the building

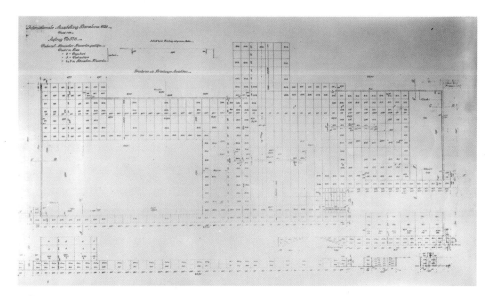

Fig. 14. Plan and elevations of the pavings and claddings supplied by Köstner und Gottschalk (1929).

of the Pavilion, extensively reproduced up until the sixties, the identification is incorrect.[19] The long, three-segmented wall which encloses the outer part of the small pool was of green Alpine marble, while the free wall by the main access steps at the entrance to the interior of the Pavilion was of the green marble from Tinos, not the other way round as is marked in the above-mentioned plan and numerous subsequent texts.

However, of the different types of stone used, the most famous is undoubtedly the *onyx doré* which Mies purchased from a Hamburg marble merchant, and from which he fashioned the free-standing central wall of the Pavilion's roofed space. Quarried, beyond all doubt, somewhere in North Africa, in Morocco, according to some authorities, or in what is now Algeria, as we believe[20], the enormous block of stone which Mies had personally set aside for the decoration of a transatlantic liner allowed him, remarkably, to design the central wall on the basis of four pieces for each face, plus a further four solid pieces forming the walls, in line with the technique adopted for all vertical stone surfaces.

16. W. Genzmer, *op. cit.*, note 9.

17. See Pere-Joan Ravetllat: «Primer van ser les parets...», in *Quaderns d'Arquitectura i Urbanisme*, n.° 163, Barcelona, 1985.

18. From a different point of view, a more critical approach to the discussion of problems of scale in Mies van der Rohe's work is offered by Tegethoff in the essay on Mies referred to above.

19. W. Genzmer, *op. cit.*, note 9.

20. The reconstruction work took us to all the onyx quarries we could find, from Egypt to Morocco, and led us to the conclusion that the onyx used by Mies must have come, virtually beyond all doubt, from one of the quarries in the Oran region of Algeria.

21. These replacement materials are referred to in the correspondence between the Pavilion authorities and Lilly Reich. Letter of the 5th of January, 1930, in the Mies van der Rohe Archive, MOMA.

22. See J. Bassegoda Nonell: «Historia y anécdota de una obra de Mies van der Rohe», in *La Vanguardia*, Barcelona, October 6th, 1979.

23. W. Blaser, *op. cit.*, note 1.

24. Report of July 8th, 1929, in the Mies van der Rohe Archive, MOMA.

Fig. 15. Detail of the meeting of the small pool with the wall and the paving.

Fig. 16. Detail of the metalwork.

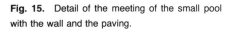

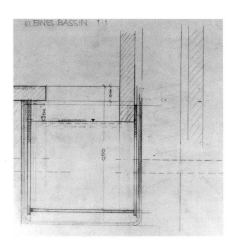

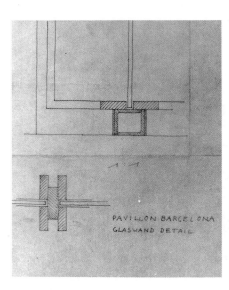

Fig. 17. Finishing the base slab.

Fig. 18. Mies during the marking out of the Pavilion.

Fig. 19. Construction of the foundations.

The figures produced by the onyx, its brilliant, diffuse coloration and its great dimensions —in slabs of 235 × 155 × 3 cm— made this naturally rich material a gem which created, perhaps more powerfully than any sculpture, a centre of interest in the flow of circulation through the building's interior.

Together with the several types of stone, we have to consider the sheets of glass of different colours and grand dimensions used in the building's plate glass walls. Clear, bottle green, mouse grey and milky white or sand-buffed, the various transparent and translucent finishes established contrasts and interplays with one another as they enclosed the limits of a single space. If we add to this the gleam of the chromed steel detailing and the undersides of the cruciform columns, and the reflective capacity of the water in the pools (fig. 15 and 16), the smaller of the two with its black glazed lining, we begin to understand that the effect of modernity and pure technology consisted not so much in the newness of the materials as in the audacious manner of their combination and the technically radical way they were used for large surfaces and simple, elemental geometric forms.

We cannot conclude this description without noting that, no doubt for economic reasons, the catalogue of materials envisaged for the building was cut back, in some cases at the last minute. While on the one hand we know that in the case of the glass and the onyx, replacements were kept in hand to make good any breakages, in the case of the green Alpine marble and the travertine the quantities ordered were reduced, with the result that the exterior side walls and the rear part of the Pavilion were not clad with these, despite the obvious need for continuity of material, but were instead built of ordinary brick, plastered and painted green and yellow, producing only the vaguest resemblance to the intended materials.

Fig. 23. Section of the column, drawn by Dirk Lohan.

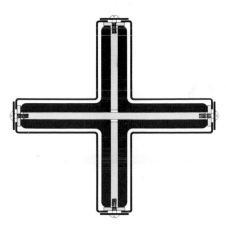

This is in all probability the reason why there are no extant photographs of the sides of the German Pavilion of 1929, and very few of the rear part. Mies himself, as well as the Exposition authorities, can have had no interest in revealing the limitations imposed by last-minute cuts in the budget on a building so admirable and so much admired by the vast majority of those who visited it.

With regard to the execution and construction techniques used on the building, we have a considerable quantity of technical details given on the plans and the descriptions and estimated costs contained in the correspondence and other documents held in the Mies van der Rohe Archive in New York.

The tradition-conscious architects of Barcelona took a certain pride in explaining that the construction of the podium base employed the time-honoured Catalan vault (fig. 17): small vaults built of brick, plastered on the narrower side, which allowed the construction of self-supporting surfaces with no need for scaffolding.[22]

The foundation system was extremely simple and superficial, based on a perimeter ditch filled with solid concrete as a support for a framework of standard-section laminated iron beams (fig. 19) on which the above-mentioned vaults rested longitudinally and to which the cruciform pillars were anchored at the appropiate points (fig. 20). The entire treatment of the podium was executed using technologies traditional to Catalonia, on a par with the construction of the roof space formed between the ceiling and roof terrace of the typical apartment building. A strong floor incorporating iron beams supports a lightweight brick structure of partition walls and a horizontal floor, also of ceramic elements, forms the so-called base on which the stone slabs rest. It is more than likely that the original construction drawings produced in Germany, of which we know nothing more than that they probably existed, proposed a different solution here, but the urgent need to complete the work in under two months, coupled with the training and resources of the Catalan builders, must have prompted the decision to proceed in this way. As far as the load-bearing structures of the walls and the two planes of the roof (fig. 21) are concerned, these were based on a framework of standard-section laminated steel beams (fig. 22). The four angles forming a cross, as in the drawing published years later in Blaser's book[23], constituted the system defining the eight pillars bearing up the roof of the Pavilion proper (fig. 23), so that instead of giving the walls a structural function, these are separated in order to show their role as purely those of enclosure and spatial division.

On top of the eight pillars there was a framework of steel beams with a depth of 210 mm which was to have formed the grid for the horizontal support of the roof. As a result of last-minute difficulties, this structure was manufactured in Barcelona[24] and its assembly (fig. 24) executed on the basis of a complex rivetting system that fixed the steel beams to the pillars by means of an octagonal plate which acted as a capital (fig. 21). There would certainly have been serious problems of sagging in the spans of more than 3 m all round the perimeter. This explains, on the one hand, the somewhat clumsy reinforcing of the cantilever section by doubling it, as well as the supplementing of the stretches adjoining the vertical supports with an extra beam with a depth of almost 300 mm. Even with these precautions, the flexibility of the structure precluded any loading of the roof, at the risk of the spans losing their horizontality and visibly increasing the sag, which explains the lightness of treatment and waterproofing of the roof. Careful scrutiny of

Fig. 20. Finishing the base slab.

Fig. 22. The metal structure of the roof during construction.

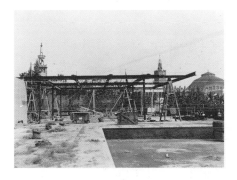

Fig. 20. Finishing the base slab.

Fig. 24. Finishing the construction.

Fig. 26. Fixing the travertine panels to the metal structure of the walls.

the documents at our disposal allows us to deduce that the roof was waterproofed on the outside, by means of parallel strips of asphalt roofing felt laid over some lightweight distributing element supported on top of the framework of beams, forming a slight incline. On the lower part, a surface of plaster and lath suspended from the roof structure formed the basis for a continuous flat ceiling, painted white. The fragility of this solution, the absence of drainage, the unforeseen slope of the roof and the problem of the sagging spans noted by more than one observer all indicate the unsatisfactory resolution of the roof of the Pavilion, and not simply because this was a temporary building. After studying the question in detail and comparing our opinions with the proposals presented in the drawing recently published by Dr Ruegenberg, we are convinced that the structural problem posited by Mies van der Rohe of a flat pavilion roof held up by a small number of local supports was no more than tentatively formulated in the case of Barcelona, and that only in the course of the entire body of his work in America, returning time and again to the problem, did Mies van der Rohe arrive at a repertoire of aesthetically and technically congruent solutions[25].

With regard to the free-standing, nonload bearing walls, the approach adopted was both novel and effective. This consisted of a framework of metal supports (fig. 26) with the slabs of travertine, marble or onyx mounted on them by means of a appropiate system of fixings. Mies applied this system, which he was later to use extensively in the United States, for the first time in the German Pavilion: it facilitated the use of stone for cladding, thanks to an undeniably new technique which avoided the problems associated with cements and stone infills, providing solutions that were not only easily dismantled but lighter and permitted the use of both sides of the material. The dismantling of these costly claddings, such as was put into practice shortly afterwards, would have proved much more problematic using the traditional fixing techniques. Undoubtedly not all of the problems posed by the borders of the surfaces sealed by a double slab were resolved, given that while Mies' solution for the lateral walls was precise and logical, with solid elements forming the entire thickness of the wall, this approach was not applied to the base, where it was not absolutely necessary, nor to the crown, where the treatment for the closure of the «sandwich» formed by the two exterior slabs was clearly resolved neither in technological nor design terms.

As for the surfaces made not of stone but of glass, extending from floor to ceiling, their characteristics are known to us by way of the detail drawings at our

Fig. 25. Study for the positioning of the slabs of green marble on the wall over the interior pool.

25. On this generic question of the resolution of the question of the Pavilion during Mies' American period, see the stimulating article by Sandra Honey: «The Office of Mies van der Rohe in America. The Towers», in *International Architect*, U.I.A., n.º 3, 1983, pp. 43-54.

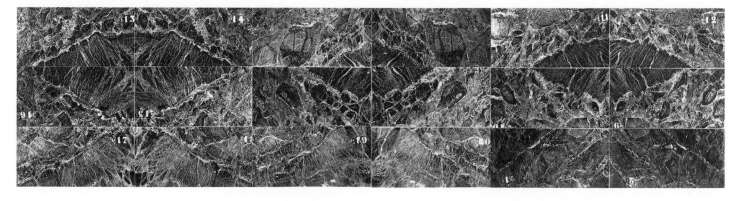

disposal (fig. 27). The general criterion here is the introduction of rigid vertical elements, sometimes of considerable depth in section, using standardized fixing. On the basis of these, which form the principal framework, a whole series of square or rectangular tubular elements are used to compose the walls, doors and windows.

Mies applied the same criterion to the design of the famous and controversial doors which served to close the building. These doors, as we can see in the relevant detail drawing (fig. 28), clearly follow the same type of division as the rest of the carpentry elements in metal, and it seems more than likely that, for all their evident necessity, they were not exactly amongst the architect's personal favourites (fig. 29). That these doors existed seems beyond question, and it takes no more than a close look at some of the period photographs to see them, or, if the doors have been removed, to discern on floor and ceiling the housings to support their upright members. It does seem to be the case that these doors could be removed without much difficulty, although it is also true that it was above all their weight and the sizeable storage space they needed that made their legendary removal each morning, only to be put back in place in the evening, so problematic...

5. Furniture

In spite of the profusion of images of the German Pavilion that have circulated since its construction, nothing has done so much to fix a lasting image of its design and ensure its continued renown as the furniture which Mies van der Rohe designed specifically for the occasion, now known by the name «Barcelona» (fig. 30).

Mies's interest in the design of furniture, and particularly of chairs, armchairs and stools, chaise-longues, etc., had intensified in the years prior to the Pavilion commission. Although he had occasionally worked on models for furniture during his apprenticeship in Berlin with Peter Behrens and Bruno Paul, it was only after the Weissenhof exhibition in Stuttgart that Mies joined in the widespread trend amongst avant-garde architects to design prototypes geared to possible industrial production. If the studios and workshops of the Bauhaus had for years been the focal point of these experiments, it is equally true that the explosion of design output from the Werkbund, Vuhtemas and Wiener Werkstätte schools provided a constant stimulus to innovation and the spread of new ideas.[26] Amongst these, none was to prove so successful as the application of the tubular metal structure to

26. See Cristopher Wilk: *Marcel Breuer. Furniture and Interiors*, New York, 1981.

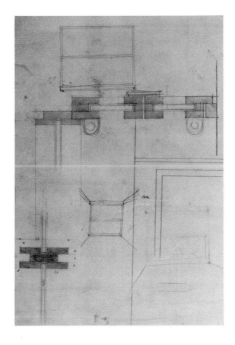

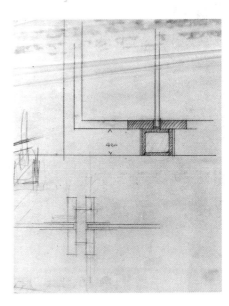

Fig. 27. Detail of the metalwork.

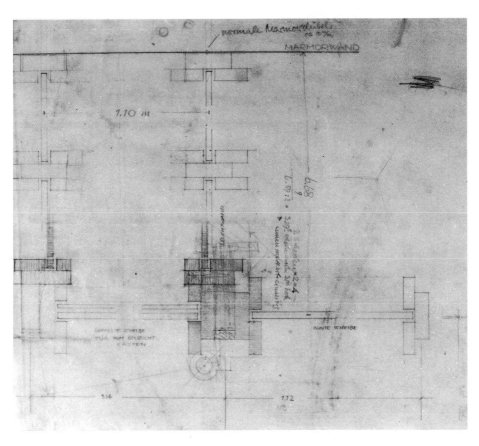

Figs. 28 and 29. Detail of the glass doors.

27. See Werner Blaser: *Mies van der Rohe. Furniture and Interiors*, London, 1982.

28. See Ludwig Glaeser: *Furniture and Furniture Drawings from the Design Collection at the Mies van der Rohe Archive*, MOMA, New York, 1977.

29. Franz Schulze: «The Barcelona Pavillon Returns», *Art in America*, vol. 67, n.º 7, November, 1979.

30. See *Exposición Internacional de Barcelona. Diario Oficial*, n.º 12, June 2nd, 1929: «Inauguración del Pabellón y Sección Alemana».

provide an aethereal, light but strong support to which seats and backs in lightweight materials could be attached. Mart Stam, Marcel Breuer and Mies himself all pioneered the design and production of chairs and armchairs in tubular steel; in 1927, after producing the M.R. prototypes for the Stuttgart exhibition, Mies was the first to patent and exploit his designs, initially for the Berlin firm of Josef Müller.[27]

In his magnificent catalogue of Mies van der Rohe's furniture designs, Ludwig Glaeser stresses the undoubted importance of the architect's professional and personal relationship with the interior designer Lilly Reich.[28] Certainly, the collaboration that had begun when both were involved in the Werkbund led the two professionals to a degree of specialization in the design of interiors,

and particularly of temporary structures for the commercial display of products in exhibitions, trade fairs and showrooms. The talent and good taste of Lilly Reich, who had trained with Hoffmann in Vienna in the 1900s, combined with Mies' rigour and refinement to produce real objects at a scale sufficiently small to allow them to be experimental and innovative in a way that might have proved impossible in production terms had they been objects of greater importance.

In the case of Barcelona, Glaeser refers in the text mentioned above to the unique character of the furniture that had to be designed. What accordingly came to be known as the «Barcelona chair», together with the corresponding ottoman stools and the two types of table designed for the same place, was not exactly furniture for mass production, but the creation of a series of ceremonial pieces designed for a very specific formal function: the inauguration of the Pavilion, and thus the opening of the space representing the new Weimar Republic at an international event in the presence of the King and Queen of Spain, who arrived in full state to preside over the ceremony.

The only two «Barcelona chairs» in existence, then, were the royal seats on which Alfonso XIII and Victoria Eugenia sat during the opening ceremony, faced by the ambassadors, ministers and other important persons in attendance. The physical framework was equally precise: sheltered by the stone canopy of the gleaming onyx wall, the two seat of honour were set apart in a space visually marked out by a great carpet of a uniform deep black. While to the right the onyx glowed with a golden sheen, to the left, by the full-height window, was the intense red of the curtain, possibly of shantung silk, hung on a moving rail mounted behind the glass. The authorities had asked that the black, red and gold colours of the German flag be present in some way; Mies decided to distribute them over three separate planes, employing the colours of the curtain, the carpet and the wall of onyx for this purpose.[29]

After the protocol speeches, the king and queen were to sign the German Pavilion's gold visitors' book and, at the end of the ceremony, join the other dignitaries in a glass of champagne. The signing ceremony and the champagne toast prompted the designing of the two tables, which were positioned next to the chairs and at the back of the enclosed area alongside the great etched glass window lit from above, respectively.[30]

The chairs and their corresponding ottomans were designed on the principle of a lightweight, almost aethereal structure on which the supporting elements rested; in this case, leather cushions for seat and, for the chairs, both seat and back. However, the structure was not in

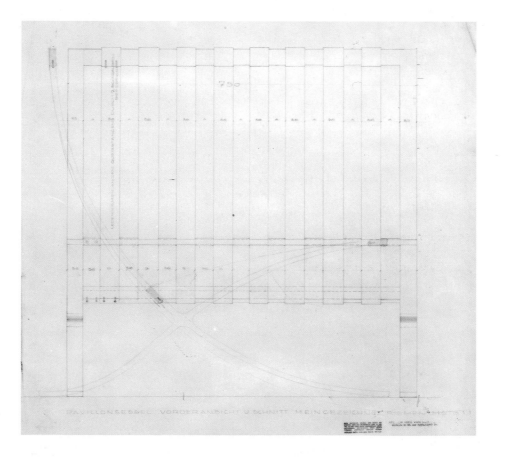

Fig. 30. Elevation and section of the Barcelona chair (1929).

this instance tubular. Starting out from the traditional scissors shape formed by the two x-shaped elements fixed and articulated at a central point, Mies designed a crosspiece composed of two solid plates which were soldered together at the mid-point to form the rigid framework by means of the meeting of two of these crosspieces with transverse braces, also of solid metal. All of the metal structural elements in the original 1929 chairs were of flexible steel, chromed and polished; the later version commercially produced by Knoll International in 1948 was of high-finish polished stainless steel. We should note here the subtle configuration of the arms of the crosspieces and the simplicity of the curving line in order to appreciate how Mies van der Rohe, starting with a regular geometrical type, introduced subtle variations into the form of the support of both chair and ottoman to improve the stability and tensile distribution. The supporting surfaces in the original version were cushions of white kidskin, upholstered in the English Chester style, which simply rested on the horizontal and vertical straps of the same hide stretched between the transverse plates of the metal structure.

Possibly one of the primary causes of the sense of lightness was the absence of a connecting rod linking the two crosspieces forming the arms to the vertical support of the structure of both chair and ottoman. Certainly such an element would have improved the structural framework, and it is relevant

here that the two table designs suffer from a degree of instability due to the lack of a connecting element to counter the effects of the heavy marble slab of the table top. This sacrifice of stability was evidently made in the interests of a lightness which, while it belonged more to the realm of appearances than reality —the «Barcelona chair» is in fact remarkably heavy— was intimately bound up with that «expression of science and technology in the present time» so passionately pursued by Mies van der Rohe as the goal of his art.[31]

We know that there was, in addition to this ceremonial furniture in the inner reception space of the Pavilion, a second set of specially designed furniture which was included in the interior of the office space. We have no photographs of these interiors, but available secondary data suggest that the offices contained a reception room, a small toilet and a second office. Thanks to the evidence of a number of photographs of the exterior, we can infer that in these offices the chairs were of the M.R. type used by Mies in various stands for the Exposition, and that they were provided here for the two or three people working in the reception and information service dealing with visitors to the Pavilion during the barely nine months of its existence. As regards this interior, we know that the floor was not of travertine, as is apparent from Köstner und Gottschalk's drawings for the cutting of the stone, and that it had its own electricity supply in addition to the water and sewage pipes for the toilet, as itemized in the surviving accounting documents.[32]

Amongst the other decorative elements which contributed to the appearance of the Pavilion were the tall masts from which the flags of Germany and Spain were flown. An imposing 15.5 m in height, these two masts were positioned symmetrically in front of the facade looking onto the Gran Plaza; the flags flying from them were also excep-

tionally large, measuring 6 × 9 m, which served to introduce elements of colour and movement that were of tremendous importance in the contrast they provided with the strict geometry and form of the Pavilion, an effect which the surviving black and white photographs at our disposal can do very little to convey.

As for the presence of floral elements, it is apparent that the large pool was planted with water lilies, which in due course covered its entire surface, even causing maintenance problems, while we know that the smaller pond did not contain any kind of vegetation. The more naturalistic treatment of the larger, more open and exposed pool, whose surface was continually ruffled by the breeze, was designed to contrast with the dark, sombre mineral severity of the enclosed area of the smaller pond, where the high walls controlled the access of daylight, creating hard, sharply defined geometries of light and shade far removed from any kind of natural vitalism.

Fig. 31. Interior showing the position of the Barcelona chairs.

31. «Our civilization depends largely on science and technology. That is the fact... The question is how far we can express that. You know, we architects are in this peculiar position. We should express the time and yet build in it. But in the end, I really believe that architecture can only be the expression of its civilization». Mies van der Rohe in Peter Blake: «A conversation with Mies», in *Four Great Makers of Modern Architecture*, Columbia University Press, New York, 1963.

32. See the Report on the costs of the Pavilion sent to Dr Schnitzler, July 15th, 1929, in the Mies van der Rohe Archive, MOMA.

Fig. 32. Turning over the site to Germany.

Fig. 33. The Pavilion seen from above.

33. See L. Glaeser: exhibition catalogue, *op. cit.*, n. 3.

34. The speech by Dr Schnitzler, German general commissioner for the Barcelona International Exposition, was a wholehearted manifestation of the New Objectivity, taking the Pavilion's formal clarity and aesthetic rigour as a metaphor for the new German spirit. «We reject everything angular, obscure, overelaborate, deadening... We want to think with clarity and rectitude. The greatest simplicity must be the proof of the greatest profundity.» The Spanish king's brief reply also took the Pavilion as a symbol, alluding to the «miracle» of the Pavilion's completion by the agreed deadline, and against all expectations, as indicative of the German people's capacity for hard work. See *Exposición Internacional de Barcelona. Diario Oficial*, n.º 12, Juny 2nd, 1929: «Inauguración del Pabellón y Sección Alemana».

It was in this second pool that Mies van der Rohe finally positioned the solitary figurative element remaining of the original intention of including three reclining statues at three different pints. The choice of the sculpture by Georg Kolbe, entitled *Dawn*, must have been made at the last moment, obtaining the piece on loan from the Berlin garden in which it had already been erected. In spite of Mies' friendship with Lehmbruck, and his admiration for Rodin, Kolbe's sculpture must have been more accessible, and possibly cheaper, than some other piece specially commissioned or chosen from a private collection. At the same time, as Ludwig Glaeser has pertinently observed, the vertical character of Kolbe's figure proved more appropriate to the vertical organization of the finishing and detailing, so that its larger-than-life dimensions and its upright position clearly contributed to making it a potent focus of visual attention at the innermost point of the Pavilion, giving the spectator approaching it an impression of gentle ascent and imposing scale.[33]

6. Maintenance and dismantling

Perhaps reading the documentation to be found in the Mies van der Rohe Archive in New York offers the best possible means of forming a clear idea of the brief life and rapid end of the German Pavilion. Up until only a few years ago, all sorts of legends circulated in Barcelona concerning the Pavilion and its fate, but we now have sufficient data to be able to describe the steps that led to its dismantling.

We can begin by affirming that construction did not properly commence before March, so that the work would have taken some three months. We know that these were months of feverish activity, and that during the last weeks up to fifty men were working round the clock in order to complete the job on time. The photographs of the construction work available to us reveal that, in the first place, the degree of mechanization was minimal, and thus that the technology employed fell far below the ideal of modernity desired by Mies. At the same time, these photographs also indicate a probably disorganized process of construction, governed by the availability of the materials from one moment to the next, so that, surprisingly, the marble walls had already been put up when the structure of the pavilion was still being built and the roofing elements were not yet in place.

The correspondence is concerned not only with the changes in the siting, but also with the strictures of the Spanish authorities, which made it necessary to rebuild the road in front of the Pavilion because of the relocation of the building at the last minute.

On the day of the inauguration, in the speech Alfonso XIII gave in reply to that of the German commissioner, the king specifically alluded, almost ironically, to German industriousness and efficiency —qualities that had been demonstrated in completing in such an incredibly short time a building such as the one he was opening.[34]

We ought to note here that, once the inauguration had been celebrated, the impression is that, as in so many other similar cases, what had not by them been completed was left undone. Anecdotally, there were a number of matters about which the organizers addressed themselves to Mies van der Rohe or to Lilly Reich indiscriminately, and these give some idea of the hasty completion and the fragile state in which the building was opened to the public: difficulties with the lighting and with the signalling on the windows, rain water, problems with the running of the curtain on its rail, doubts about the positioning of the furniture, and so on.

At the beginning of July, both Lilly Reich and Mies were in Berlin, after spending a few days relaxing in Biarritz. The postal communications continued, but there is no evidence that either of them ever saw their building again.

When, early in 1930, the question of the Pavilion's future was raised, the correspondence reveals that various different solutions were suggested. In the first place, the sale of the building. This was the approach adopted with many of the national pavilions, a number of which were bought by public or private interests, and, where the building allowed, were remodelled or physically moved to suit the uses envisaged by the new owners. Schools, warehouses and homes were the final destiny of pavilions such as those of Sweden, Denmark, Belgium, the Philippines Tobacco Company and others. Some similar solution would no dobut have been considered for the German Pavilion. We know that the German authorities were negotiating with a Barcelona businessman who was interested in turning the building into a restaurant. For some reason, no agreement was reached, possibly because the entrepreneur wanted to rent the building while the Germans were only interested in selling it.[35] In the end, it was decided to dismantle the construction. The company that had supplied the marble, Köstner und Gottschalk, took charge of it for possible reuse. The chromed steel structures were also sent back to Berlin for a possible reutilization or resale, to help offset the deficit created by the Pavilion. The steel structure was sold off for scrap in Barcelona, and was almost certainly the only part of the building to remain —but now unrecognizable— in the city.[36] The unobtrusive foundations were covered over by a modest garden, planted with palm trees, which must have been laid out after the Civil War, and remained that way for more than fifty years. A small piece of the onyx did service as a table top in Dr Ruegenberg's home in Berlin; in Mies' apartment in Chicago, the metal structure from one of the ottoman stools supported a slab of marble to provide an occasional table. Philip C. Johnson, the first American admirer of the work of Mies van der Rohe, managed to acquire one of the armchairs to enrich his collection of 20th century art.

35. Letter to Lilly Reich, dated December 29th, 1929, in the Mies van der Rohe Archive, MOMA.

36. Letter to Mies van der Rohe, March 5th, 1930, in the Mies van der Rohe Archive, MOMA.

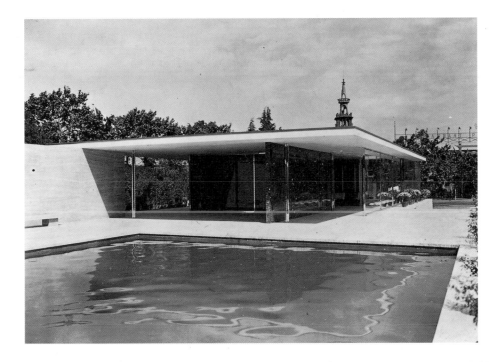

Fig. 34. The Pavilion with the large pool.

Fig. 35. View of the exterior with the Palau de Victòria Eugènia in the background.

Fig. 36. View of the rear access.

Fig. 37. View from the service annexes.

Fig. 39. View towards the small pool by the onyx wall.

Fig. 38. View towards the service annexes.

Fig. 40. Perspective of the sculpture by G. Kolbe.

Fig. 42. Interior sculpture.

Fig. 41. One of the onyx doors of the Pavilion.

Fig. 44. Entering the Pavilion.

Fig. 45. Interior.

Fig. 43. View of the interior with the onyx wall and black carpet.

Fig. 47. The day of the inauguration.

Fig. 46. King Alfonso XIII by the small pool.

Fig. 48. King Alfonso XIII in front of the light wall.

II. The reconstruction of the German Pavilion in Barcelona: 1981-1986

1. Antecedents

The idea of reconstructing the German Pavilion built for the Barcelona International Exposition of 1929 goes back quite a number of years.

We know that as early as 1959, Grup R, through its secretary, Oriol Bohigas, contacted the architect Mies van der Rohe to propose the rebuilding of the Pavilion. The correspondence relating to this initiative is still extant, as is the affirmative response of the Pavilion's architect accepting both the idea as such and the responsibility of taking charge of the work, without fee. However, the lack of support from official bodies for the proposal left the initiative in limbo.

Sometime in 1964 the architect Juan Bassegoda Nonell had a plan drawn up and a schematic model made, which he duly presented to José Maria de Porcioles, then mayor of Barcelona, with the intention of reconstructing the Pavilion, but this, too, proved fruitless.

In 1974, the architect Fernando Ramos organized a seminar in the Escola Tècnica Superior d'Arquitectura de Barcelona in order to study the construction problems presented by the building and to promote understanding and analysis both of the vanished monument and of the continually recurring idea of its possible reconstruction.

In 1978, in Barcelona itself, we were able to talk to Ludwig Glaeser, at that time curator of the Mies van der Rohe Archive of the Museum of Modern Art in New York, who was then preparing an exhibition for the following year, the fiftieth anniversary of the Pavilion. Ignasi de Solà-Morales had a series of meetings with Glaeser, the outcome of which was an agreement for the mutual exhange of documentary materials and the combining of his and our efforts.

Solà-Morales reciprocated by organizing a seminar at the Escola d'Arquitectura devoted to reviewing the entire body of data relating to the 1929 International Exposition, and this in turn re-sulted in a series of publications and conferences, and an exhibition at the Fundació Miró in January 1980 which included as one of its elements the exhibition that Glaeser had been preparing for the United States, with original documentary material and a virtually exhaustive summary of the available information on the German Pavilion.

In 1981, the architect Oriol Bohigas, on being appointed to the post of director of Urbanism and Building by Barcelona City Council, revived the initiatve with an agreement between the then mayor, Narcis Serra, and the president of the International Trades Fair, Josep Maria Figueras. The result of this was that we, the authors of this book, were commissioned to produce the scheme that was finally built, at the same time organizing contacts within Spain and internationally to ensure that the project was carried out with the greatest degree of scientific rigour and acceptance by informed opinion in the fields of architecture and contemporary art.

Perhaps one of Oriol Bohigas' most telling perceptions was the intuition that the reconstruction, the documentary and economic problems associated with which were of mythic status, could only be carried forward if a project was commissioned; that is, first of all a process of analysis, determining dimensions and techniques, which would let us know down to the last detail what was the true scale of the difficulties posed by the reconstruction.

The problem with the project was, of course, of a very special kind. As soon as we set to work we realized that the plans published up to then by biographers and scholars of Mies van der Rohe contained significant differences in dimensions and in detailing.

It proved necessary to reconstruct the entire process, beginning with the successive versions of the Pavilion in the plans in the possession of the various centres of documentation, above all the Mies van der Rohe Archive at the MOMA in New York, and going on to the different attempts at redrawing, in particular of the plan of the building, undertaken by a succession of Mies scho-

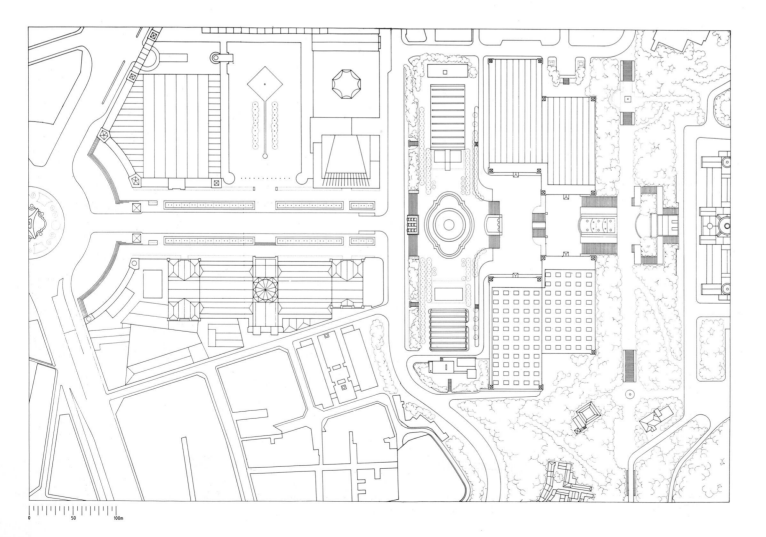

Fig. 49. The Pavilion in the context of the Fira de Barcelona precinct, during construction.

lars, such as Walter Genzmer (1929), Rubió i Tudurí (1929), Philip Johnson (1932, 1947), Bruno Zevi (1948), Ludwig Hilberseimer (1956), Arthur Drexler (1960), Werner Blaser (1965), Ludwig Glaeser (1969, 1977 and 1979), David A. Spaeth (1979) and Wolf Tegethoff (1981).

After consulting the most important archives, such as the MOMA, the Stiftung Preussischer Kulturbesitz in Berlin or the Institut Municipal d'Història de Barcelona, and establishing contacts with scholars such as Oriol Bohigas, Juan Bassegoda, Ludwig Glaeser, Arthur Drexler, Dirk Lohan, Sergius Ruegenberg and others, as well as with architects who had seen or had some relationship with the building, such as Josep Lluís Sert, Joan Baptista Subirana, Nicolau M.ª Rubió i Tudurí, Àngel Truñó and Buenaventura Bassegoda Musté, we were in a position to draw one or two conclusions.

The first was that the nonexistence, possibly absolute, of *a project* had been responsible for the differences between the sets of drawings published over a period of more than fifty years. Mies van der Rohe had produced a series of drawings that were transformed and adapted under the tremendous pressure of the haste with which the work had to be carried out. Changes in the budget, conditions imposed by the technology available in Barcelona at that time, hold-ups in the delivery of some of the materials and mistakes in the original survey of the topography obliged the architect to make adjustments and changes up to the very last moment, so that what constitutes the body of our knowledge today, with certain gaps and lacunae, are the process and the characteristics of the building at each stage of its evolution. In understanding this process, we also possess the knowledge needed to understand and appreciate the contributions made and, it must be said, the confusions created by most of the versions of the plan or of certain specific details published over the years.

In carrying out the brief for the project given us we were fortunate to have the assistance of the architects Virginia Figueras and Claudia Mann. For the calculation of quantities, dimensions and budgets, we had the help of the clerks of works J. Barrena and R. Ayala, who subsequently shared in the supervision on site, to which the young architect Isabel Bachs also made a valuable contribution.

The drawing up of the project and the quantifying of the budget, which initially came to 105,337,446 pesetas, made it possible to arrive at two definitive conclusions. The first was that reconstruction was feasible from the documentary point of view, that is, it was possible to work out exactly the characteristics of the building conceived and built by Mies van der Rohe. The second conclusion was that the cost of reconstruction was acceptable. Arthur Drexler, when he heard the estimated cost, exclaimed «It's a bargain!». Although it was a sizeable sum in terms of the public resources of the time, it was clearly understood that reconstruction was technically and economically viable. The design project had fixed the parameters of the problem. The next stage was to set up a procedure in order to carry out the construction work.

On the 10th of October, 1983, with Pasqual Maragall —the new mayor of Barcelona on Narcis Serra's appointment as Spain's Minister of Defence —as president, the Fundació Pública del Pabelló Alemany de Barcelona— Mies van der Rohe was formally constituted: invited onto the Fundació were the Ajuntament de Barcelona, the Fira de Mostres de Barcelona, the Museum of Modern Art of New York, the Stiftung Preussischer Kulturbesitz of Berlin and the Escola Tècnica Superior d'Arquitectura de Barcelona. The individuals who at that time represented these bodies were: for the Fira de Barcelona, Josep Maria Figueras, as president, with the members of the executive committee, Raimon Martínez Fraile and Germà Vidal; Arthur Drexler, as head of the Architecture and Design section of the

Fig. 50. The Pavilion in the context of the Fira de Barcelona precinct, from a proposal for the refurbishment of the area by Ignasi de Solà-Morales.

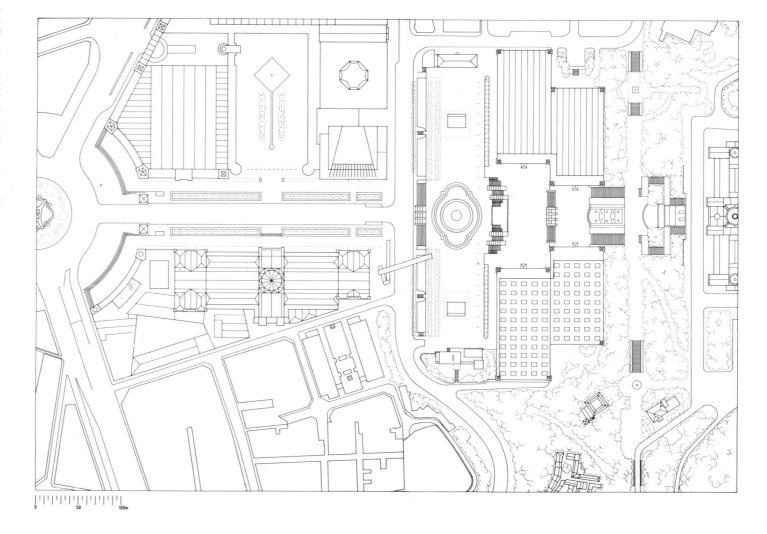

MOMA; Wolf Dietler-Dube, as director of Museums of the Stiftung Preussischer Kulturbesitz; Josep Muntañola, as director of the Escola d'Arquitectura de Barcelona; Jordi Parpal and Maria Aurelia Capmany, representing the Ajuntament. The Fundació was constituted in the Saló de Cròniques of the Ajuntament de Barcelona, and that same day saw the ceremonial laying of the first stone of the future reconstruction. At the same time the Fundació Mies van der Rohe appointed a Committee of Experts, whose task was to supervise the project and the execution of the building. This Committee was made up of Josep Maria Figueras, Oriol Bohigas, Richard Oldenburg, Arthur Drexler, Dirk Lohan, Julius Possener, Cristian Cirici, Fernando Ramos, Ignasi de Solà-Morales and Josep Miquel Abad.

2. The design process

The first question raised by the reconstruction was that of the location of the building.

There was a widely received idea, very much in line with the interpretation of Mies' architecture in the fifties, that saw the Barcelona Pavilion as a prototype; a perfect, autonomous spatial experiment capable of being considered as an object. Given the terms of this logic, it was by no means strange that for many people it made little or no difference whether it was rebuilt in Barcelona or in Bologna, Frankfurt or Berlin. A more detailed, more rigurous knowledge of the Pavilion clearly revealed to us the building's total relationship with the site that Mies himself had chosen for it. The relationship with the other buildings, the Gran Plaza, the ascent from this to the hill of the Pueblo Español, the topography, were all aspects of the basic premises of the project, without which the building was stripped of all its meaning. For this reason the

site shosen for the reconstruction of the German Pavilion was precisely the spot occupied by the original in 1929-1930. This was a plot of land, roughly in the shape of a half moon, bounded by a rectilinear road which ran as far as the north facade of the Palau de Victòria Eugenia, and by a second curving, ascending road which ran from the main avenue to give access to the rear, and higher, part of the Palau de Victòria Eugenia.

This plot comprises a relatively level space fronting the first of these roads, and a sloping area corresponding to the curving road to the rear.

The vegetation we found on the site was basically the same as had been there at the time of the Exposition, with the enormous difference of the tremendous growth of the trees in the intervening years.

It should be noted that the position of the Pavilion must be seen in relation to the layout of intermediary platform as a whole, created by the system of steps ascending from the site of the 1929 Exposition to the crowning point of the Palau Nacional.

The esplanade on which the German Pavilion stood is centred on the great monumental fountain, with its changing jets of water and coloured lighting, designed by the engineer Carles Buigas. Alongside this there were two other, smaller, symmetrically placed fountains, and at the end of the esplanade, following the transverse axis, a group of free-standing Ionic columns which had formed the boundary between the Exposition area and the gardens. Behind these columns, positioned symmetrically, were the German Pavilion to the west and the Pavilion of the City of Barcelona, still standing today, on the opposite side.

The subsequent construction of a pavilion for the Instituto Nacional de Industria (INI) to the west, the removal of the colonnade and various changes to the landscaping and the fountains had all significantly altered the aspect of this

part of the site. It was evident that with the removal of the INI pavilion and the restoring of certain elements of the gardens to their original state, it would be fairly easy to recover the former appearance of this open space.

At the same time, a superficial excavation of the site laid bare the foundations of the 1929 building. Thus the discovery of the original situation, to say nothing of the obvious subjective value of these remains, provided us with an important source of information. In the first place, as a basis for determining the overall dimensions of the building, a factor intimately related to the modulation of its construction elements; and secondly, in reference to its precise position and its relationship to the Gran Plaza, the flight of steps to the rear, the Palau de Victòria Eugenia and the trees occupying the area to the back of the plot.

Nevertheless, the conditions presented by the site were not in themselves sufficient to guide the evolution of the project. As we have already noted, the information at our disposal inevitably led us to a process of interpretation of the data and the determining of a series of priority criteria.

No reconstruction can avoid acknowledging the existence of certain specific criteria, according to which the problems it poses are resolved. In the case of the reconstruction of the German Pavilion, the criteria were not drawn up in isolation, but in an attempt to balance the various different interests to be satisfied by the project as a whole. For this reason, we would like to explain these criteria, while making it clear that the order in which they are set out here does reflect in some way an order of priority.

Fig. 51. Discovery of the foundations of the 1929 Pavilion. The anchoring of a metal pillar.

Fig. 52. Remains of a metal pillar found in the subsoil of the Pavilion. Its form and dimensions made it possible to determine the solution actually employed in 1929.

There was never at any time any idea of a conceptual revision of the original project; rather, an undisputed premise here was the concept of a reconstruction that would interpret as faithfully as possible the idea and the material form of the 1929 Pavilion. If we have made a distinction between idea and material form, it is because the study of the materials used in the project, alongside other contemporary schemes by its architect, indicates that the physical execution of the building, for reasons of economy, haste or simple technological limitations, did not always come up to the level of its ideal character before, during and after construction.

Our fidelity to Mies van der Rohe's idea was by no means gratuitous or merely speculative, but was contrasted point by point with the available information on the concrete solutions employed in the original building.

The reconstruction was thus undertaken not in order the raise anew a building following exactly the same technical conditions of the 1929 Pavilion, but with a view to guaranteeing its permanence. Certain problems with the solidity of the roof, with rain water drainage, with services and security were approached in quite a different way in the light of the experience of the durability of the Pavilion constructed by Mies van der Rohe.

Accordingly, without presuming to change either the conception or the appearance of the building, it was to some extent necessary to redesign some of the detailing, and in those instances what we looked for was to achieve greater architectonic coherence and remain faithful to the design logic of the building itself.

The problem of durability is intimately related to the use to be made of the building, as a guarantee of its appearance and maintenance. Two significant measures have been adopted to this end, namely the setting up of a Board

of Trustees with direct responsibility for the administration and upkeep of the building, and its immediate classification as a monument; moreover, it should be pointed out that the building was designed for a function similar to that of the original. It is to be used as a representative space, for visiting and meeting in, where a number of people can gather to celebrate social of official occasions

For the Fira Internacional de Mostres de Barcelona or the City Council, the Pavilion can be used as a symbolic venue in which to hold openings, presentations and other formal social events. Thus the furnishing and fitting out of the building has been kept to a minimum, amounting to no more than the equipping of the interior of the smaller volume as an office.

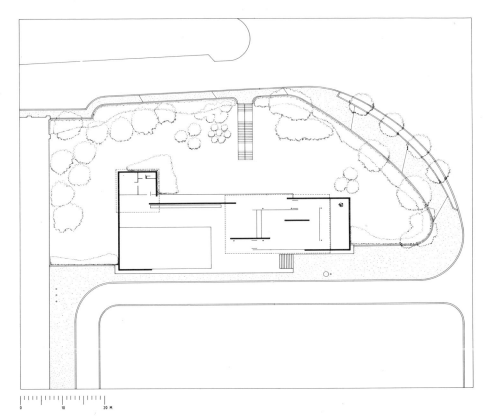

Fig. 53. General plan and landscaping.

Fig. 54. Plan of the reconstructed Pavilion.

Fig. 55. Roof plan.

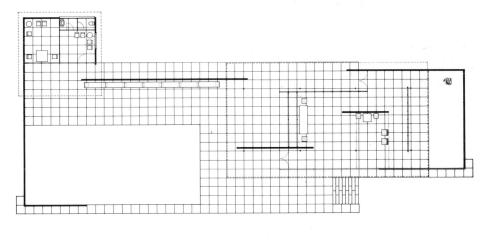

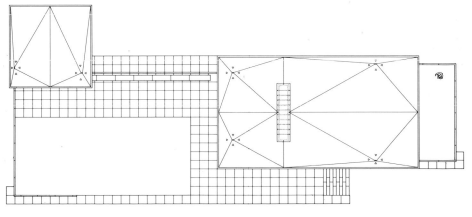

Fig. 56. East and west elevations.

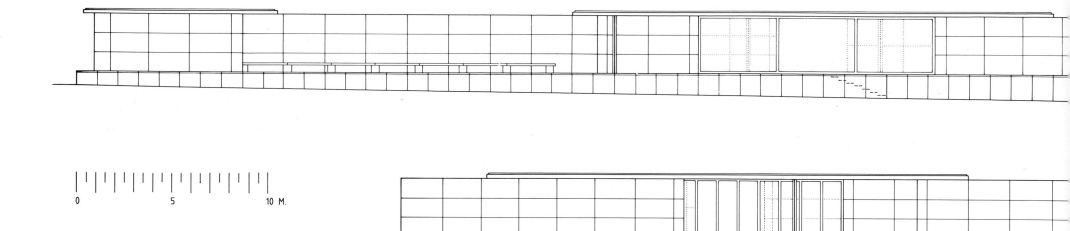

0   5   10 M.

Fig. 58. The travertine cut in the form of the cladding slabs.

Fig. 59. The blocks of travertine for the Pavilion in the quarry in Tivoli.

The original Pavilion was designed to be a fluid space, open to the road and the garden. It was only after its inauguration that Mies designed doors for his building, whose incorporation has an evident air of being something additional.

In the reconstruction project, these doors have again been included, and for the same reasons. The security of the reconstructed building is based on two systems: a combined system with an alarm to detect intruders and a special external lighting system which allows constant surveillance throughout the night.

3. The materials

The travertine
Our commitment to understanding the architecture as an expression of the essence with the construction techniques and systems, makes the selection of the materials for the Pavilion of particular critical interest, in that Mies'

work sets out to be the expression of the material and the systems used in its construction. The choice of these is thus the key to the definition of Mies van der Rohe's architectonic will.

The attempt to understand any architecture necessarily calls for analysis of the elements employed in its construction, but in the present case this approach needs to be particularly acute. It would be particularly inconsistent to neglect such an analysis in considering Mies' architecture. As Mies himself said in 1924, «architecture is the will of an age translated into space. Until this elementary truth is admitted, the new architecture will be changing and experimental. Until then it will be a chaos of uncontrolled forces. What is primordial is to resolve the question of the nature of architecture. It is necessary to believe that this is intimately related to the spirit of its time, that it can only manifest itself in vital activities and in the context of its time. It has never been otherwise.»

In the Pavilion, particular attention should be given to the marble and its treatment, working and positioning, since it constitutes the greater part of both the surface area and the budget, as well as formally determining the basic appearance of the building.

Four different types of marble were used in the Barcelona Pavilion: Roman travertine, green marble from the Alps, old green marble from Greece and onyx from the Atlas.

Of these four types of stone, the one that most clearly marks out the image of the Pavilion is the travertine, used for the exterior walls and the paving.

The knowledge we have of the characteristics of the 1929 Pavilion is set out on page 13.

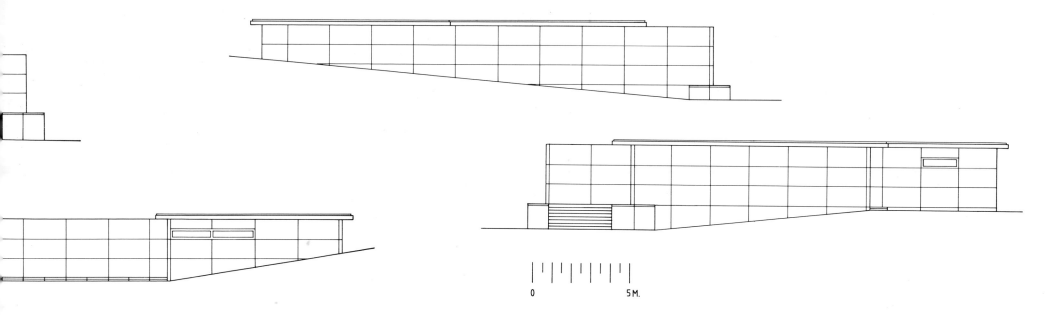

Fig. 57. South and north elevations.

| | | | | | | |
0   5 M.

In selecting the travertine for the reconstruction, we decided on stone for the walls from the «Colosseo» quarry in Bagni di Tivoli, in the Lazio region. There we looked for a block with the same irregular dip that had originally suggested to Mies the composition of the wall behind the continuous bench. The face of this block was pitted with little holes, and this, combined with its not being horizontal, meant that the owner of the quarry, Sig. Conversi, was extremely satisfied with our choice, which took what he felt to be a distinctly second-rate block of material off his hands. And, from the ordinary viewpoint, it was second-rate stone, just as the stone used in the original 1929 Pavilion had been. We decided not to fill in the little holes on the surface, which exposed the internal structure of the travertine, consisting of little fossil spheres corresponding to the gas bubbles produced around the nodules of vegetable matter during the stone's formation, and since fossilized, carbonized or vanished, leaving residues diffused throughout the material.

This material, essential to the faithful reconstruction of the walls, was entirely unsuitable, on account of its pitted surface and irregular pattern, for the paving slabs, We therefore decided to try the other quarries in the vicinity for a travertine of similar composition but greater compaction, and thus greater density and better mechanical characteristics. Given that the irregularities corresponded to the edges of the lakeside area, we had to travel only a short distance to find a travertine with far better characteristics for our purposes, in the «Sybilla» quarry, also in Tivoli.

In order to obtain the right composition, our project included drawings detailing the cutting of the blocks, giving a number to each block in turn which was then assigned to its appointed position in the wall, so that the rhombic composition of the travertine in the wall behind the bench was made quite explicit. Probably on account of the unusual nature of our desire to compose the pattern of the travertine, neither suppliers nor intermediaries proved capable of interpreting the project, and shipped the material all mixed together and out of sequence.

Thanks to the sensibility and dedication which our marble mason —Jordi Marqués, from Granollers— and his men brought to the working of the travertine, and the patience with which all of the technical team accepted the need to put together and change as many times as necessary this jigsaw puzzle in travertine, we managed to achieve the desired result after rearranging the cladding four times.

Fig. 60. Anchoring piece with triple movement for adjusting height, width and depth.

The other stone materials used were the two types of green marble: one for the walls surrounding the internal pond —Alpine green marble— and one for the principal point of entry into the interior of the building —green marble from Tinos.

The first of these comes from the quarries of the Valle d'Aosta. Frequently used by Mies in subsequent buildings, the stone is characterized by its pattern of white veining over a vivid bluey green. In this case, just as Mies had done for the 1929 building, the combination of successive cuts were placed in a symmetrical arrangement, in groups of four slabs, to form the great concentric figures which create the spectacular effect of a vast landscape. On this occasion, the working out in advance the precise distribution of the pieces made it possible to form the figures on the interior as well as the exterior face of the wall. It should be noted here that it was our firm decision to totally clad all three faces of this wall, although we were well aware that on the 1929 building two of the exterior wall surfaces were without the green marble, which was replaced by a simple rendering in the same tone as the stone.

In this respect, too, we were perfectly clear that our criterion was not to reproduce the building as it had actually been when it was completed —or not completed— in 1929, but to carry through to its conclusion an idea with regard to which we had an abundance of information and the support of an architectural logic that was beyond all doubt.

As far as the green marble from Tinos is concerned, this is quarried in the region of Larissa, in Greece, and is thus also known as Larissa green marble. It is worth noting here that we were led to conclude that very many publications dealing with the Barcelona Pavilion perpetuate what we believe to be a confusion, originating in the description Genzmer published in 1929, wrongly referring to the Tinos green marble as Alpine green marble, and vice versa.

This Tinos or Larissa marble is a calcareous stone, its background colour a deep green verging on black, with highly irregular incrustations of stronger co-

lours, frequently white, silver, black and violet. The absolutely irregular distribution of these different colours, which do not appear in continuous veins, did not suggest an overall ordering composition of the slabs in any sequence. Instead, the slabs have been simply positioned so as to create a random pattern of shapes and colours which is singularly pleasing to the eye.

Finally, the most luxurious cladding material used in the building is the onyx, eight large slabs of which cover the free-standing wall in the central part of the Pavilion, as a finishing over the solid masonry core, using the same technique employed for the other stone walls.

Mies' onyx was familiar to us from various graphic and written descriptions, as well as by comparison with the extant cladding on the Tugendhadt house in Brno. Mies had purchased several blocks from a Hamburg supplier who had them set aside for the decoration of a transatlantic liner. They probably

Fig. 61. The process of positioning the travertine slabs.

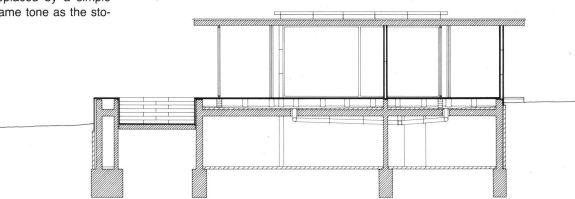

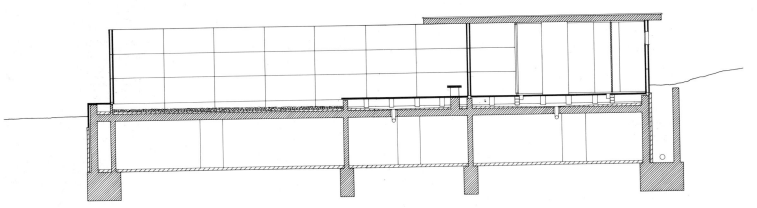

Fig. 62. Section of the main building.

Fig. 63. Section of the auxiliary building.

0   5 M.

32

came from one of the quarries then being worked in the French colony of Morocco.

The search for a similar material constituted the most novelesque episode in the entire process of reconstructing the Pavilion. After endless inquiries of all the usual suppliers of this material, and in the knowledge that the dimensions we needed for the wall were very much greater than whatever was available on the market, we decided to go directly to the sources which seemed most likely to be able to provide what we were looking for. Israel, Egypt, Brazil, Pakistan were all initial possibilities which proved fruitless in view of the apparently absurd size of the slabs we needed.

Finally, it was in the abandoned quarry of Bou-Hanifia, in what is now Algeria, that Fernando Ramos and Jordi Marqués discovered the material with large enough dimensions and similar characteristics to the legendary *onyx doré* of he 1929 Pavilion.

Our work with the stone elements proved to be an extremely interesting experience. Since nature never produces two identical stones, not even in the same quarry, our task as reconstructors was equally divided between a faithful adherence to the colour, texture and shine of the material and our creative capacity to act as architects interpreting what was, in our judgement, Mies' intention at the moment of choosing the material, the cut and the finish. This tension between imitation and invention was what marked out our work as being not a mere process of restitution but a genuine project.

4. Construction of the building

The base of the building consists of the foundations, the retaining walls, the structure of elevation on the site and the floor slab, together with the paving with which this is covered. We shall proceed to analyze these elements one by one.

The foundations of the 1929 building were continuous strip trenches filled with ordinary concrete. We had fairly clear ideas about the constitution of the foundations from various period photographs, but it was nonetheless tremendously gratifying for us to remove a shallow layer of earth and find, by means of regularly spaced trenches, in the traditional archaelogical fashion, the entire foundations of the old Pavilion.

However, nothing had survived of the brickwork vaults of the floor slab of the original Pavilion.

In consequence of our decision to incline this floor slab to provide drainage, we chose to construct a conventional unidirectional slab, above which were the slopes, damp-proof course, a layer of mortar for protection and, on top of this and supported at the centre and the four corners, leaving a drainage chamber, the travertine slabs, 5 cm thick, measuring 1.09 × 1.09 m. We were thus able to avoid the problem of puddles forming, an inherent risk in any entirely horizontal surface exposed to the weather. In this way we also managed to ventilate the chamber beneath the floor used for the routing and control of the services in the interior of the base, comprising the filter for the water in the pools, a small heating unit for the offices, the electrical and drainage services, and the computer, telephone and security alarm systems with which the Pavilion offices were equipped.

The retaining walls are of reinforced concrete. In the corner by the highest part of the site the excavation of the foundations revealed that Mies had applied the same solution we had decided

on: the construction of a retaining wall to hold back the earth in the corner, free-standing and separated from the office building by one metre, so that any deformation of the wall by earth pressure would not affect our structure, as well as to create a drainage zone, filling the cavity between the wall and the building with stones and incorporating the necessary conduits for the water thus drained.

The walls
Mies attached considerable importance to the freeing of the walls from their traditionally primary function: load bearing.

Released from the function of supporting the roof, Mies' walls were free to carry out their other tasks: separating, defining spaces, marking out itineraries and presenting to touch and sight their patterns, colours and textures. The stone is thus liberated, from now on, from its structural task and confirmed in its role of cladding the walls.

In these free-standing walls continuity and support are provided by an orthogonal network of U-sectioned metal elements which make up frames which are spaced at the same interval as the module used for the stone slabs. The slabs which cover both of the wall surfaces are fixed to this metal framework with a continuous butt joint, the better to express, in its patent defiance of the laws governing conventional tongued and grooved joints, the fact that here the stone is being used as a cladding material, on the walls (30 mm thick) as well as the floor (50 mm thick).

The solution adopted was both novel and effective: a framework of metal supports on which the travertine, marble or onyx slabs are mounted by means of a suitable system of fixings. In the Pavilion, Mies van der Rohe first tested this system which he was later to introduce to the United States, and which allowed the use of the stone as a cladding material thanks to an unquestionably new technique that was free of the problems associated with

Fig. 64. Tests for the support of the suspended flooring.

Fig. 65. Preparation of the anchoring slots on the edges of the travertine slabs.

Fig. 66. Detail of the anchoring of the slabs to the metal supporting structure.

cladding based on cements and stone infills, permitting solutions that were not only easy to dismantle but both lighter and reversible in their use of the material. The possibility of dismantling these costly finishes, as was subsequently carried out, would have been much more difficult using traditional cladding techniques. It is nevertheless true that not all of the problems posed by the edges of the surfaces covered by double slabs were resolved, given that while on the side walls Mies applied a precise, logical solution using solid elements of the same thickness as the wall, this was not extended to the base, where it was not essential, nor to the crown, where the solution consisted of a sandwich composed of the two outer slabs in a way that was unsatisfactory in terms of both design and technology.

Certain of these problems, together with apprehension about the effects of Barcelona's maritime, industrial climate on a metal structure that could not be inspected and overhauled, meant that our decision as to the system to be adopted in the reconstruction of the walls passed through various different stages.

Originally, our concern with durability, together with the fact that Mies had filled the cavities between the metal framework and the stone cladding with mortar, led us to think that we might perhaps obtain better resistance to the unquestionably corrosive maritime and industrial atmosphere of Montjuïc, given the real evidence of the backing-up, with a wall that was itself of stone or reinforced concrete. That was our first proposal. Later we came to see that one of the reasons for backing up the cavities had been the little-known fact that, in consequence of the cutbacks in the budget imposed on the project, only those surfaces which gave onto the interior of the Pavilion or the main facade

Fig. 67. Fixing the slabs of Alpine green marble in place.

Fig. 68. The slabs of Alpine green marble with their identification numbers.

were clad in stone, while the others were rendered and then painted to give a degree of chromatic continuity with the material used to clad the corresponding wall.

Evidently, the need to provide a continuous base for the plaster rendering was a more than sufficient motive for the general backing-up. Since this problem was not one which our project had to address, we chose to return to the concept of a load-bearing metal framework with the cladding fixed to it, thus allowing freedom of movement to the various panels, which rested entirely on the four points provided by the system of fixing, without suffering constraint from a concrete infill which might also in due course include other kinds of geological movement.

This decision was also influenced by seeing the continuing viability of the solution originally proposed by Mies for the stone cladding and subsequently adopted by P.C. Johnson in his New York skyscraper for AT&T. The decision to rest the stone slabs on only four points called for great care in the design of the system of fixings holding them in place.

Starting with a system of anchors manufactured by the German company Frimeda, with additional input from the Spanish firm Mecanotubos, slight modifications were made in order to facilitate the placing of the fixings on the sides of the panels, as is normally the case, or at top and bottom, where the construction process required this. The thickness of the fixing panel was also adjusted so as to show the desired thickness of the joints (5 mm).

The load-bearing structure, roofs and waterproofing
The load-bearing structure of the roofs was approached differently in each case. While the roof of the office building rests on the metal framework of the walls, the roof of the main volume of the Pavilion is supported on eight cruciform-section pillars, which form four symmetrical bays, with a central space of 6.65 × 7.35 m and a span at the edges of 2.10 × 3.45 m.

The discovery inside a foundation trench of the anchoring for one of the pillars enabled us to correct an error in our dimensions: the L-shaped members of the cross-section, which in our project, based on the authority of a number of studies, measured 100 × 100 × 8 mm, in fact measured 100 × 100 × 10 mm in the original.

We felt it would be ill-advised to literally repeat a construction system for the roof which Mies himself had modified in subsequent schemes. At the same time, the considerable spans of the roof demanded a structural element that would not readily suffer from metal corrosion. After a stage during which our project proposed a reticular concrete slab for the roof, we decided to simplify this, opting instead for a continuous reinforced concrete slab to avoid problems of differing degrees of adherence in the covering of the roof.

In order to prevent the deformation of the points of the slab, the concrete form has been constructed with a contraflexure of the order of 6 cm.

As far as the waterproofing is concerned, while the structure of the roofs has been resolved using a variety of construction techniques, its geometry, after lengthy debate, was not altered, so that there is a system of direct rainwater drainage for the entire perimeter of the roof slabs. This, combined with the slight slope of the slab, led us to replace the bitumen felts used on the roof of the original Pavilion with strengthened grey polyester, thus avoiding joins, which are apt to leak where the slope is very slight, and facilitating subsequent maintenance.

The woodwork and metalwork
The metalwork on the window fames of the building was familiar to us from the details recently discovered amongst a collection of other papers on the Barcelona Pavilion in the Mies van der Rohe Archive at the MOMA, New York.

We have respected the original characteristics of this metalwork detailing, except in the use of chrome for the finishing. Numerous tests carried out using the best techniques led us to the conclusion that, given the acidity and humidity of the Barcelona climate, it was impossible to guarantee an acceptable durability for this finish. The metalwork used in the reconstructed Pavilion is thus entirely of polished stainless steel, giving a brilliant finish which closely resembles the mirror-like shine of the chrome used in 1929.

It has proved highly instructive to analyze the succession of Mies' metalwork detailing throughout the course of his architectural career and discover that Mies remained faithful to the end to the scheme he had worked out for the Pavilion, not only in his smaller buildings but in the skyscrapers, despite the fact that these called for much greater rigour to ensure the sealing of the joints.

The woodwork in the interior of the administrative offices follows the distribution most probably established by Mies, although it is not entirely certain that this interior was properly finished. We have used wooden frames dressed with clear varnished maple panelling to form the interior divisions and the doors communicating the two offices and the toilet in the service pavilion. These are the only wood finishes anywhere in the Barcelona Pavilion, and their design, although based on an analysis of the way such divisions using wooden frames and panels are typically handled in later buildings by Mies van der Rohe, is the product of project criteria established by the architects responsible for the reconstruction.

Security and the surrounding area
The maintenance of the building, and above all its security, pose the same problems today as they did in the past. Mies van der Rohe created a building conceptually linked to a continuous circulation route in which there was no precise impassable barrier between the exterior and the interior. However, while there was no need to restrict the free

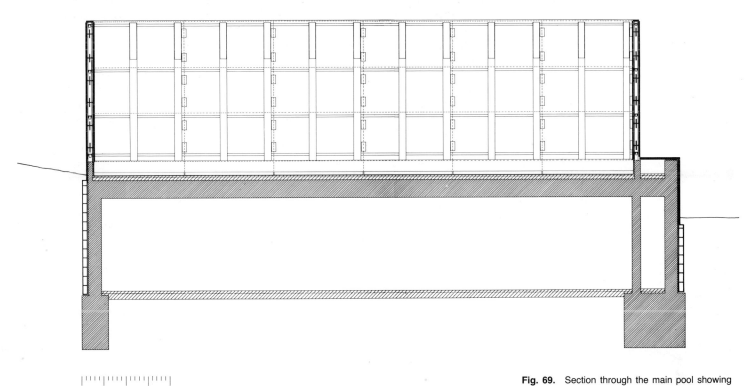

Fig. 69. Section through the main pool showing the load-bearing metal structure of the travertine walls.

movement of visitors around the exterior space, the interior, with its furnishings and delicate finishes, presented obvious problems of control.

The same solution has been adopted for the reconstruction as for the original building. Mies designed doors which could be easily removed and replaced as circumstances demanded. These two double doors, whose metal construction is similar to that of the large windows, with clear glass, have been recreated in their original form. There are extant working details, filed by mistake amongst other projects in the Mies van der Rohe Archive in the MOMA and recently rediscovered. The technical solution did not present any great difficulties, bearing in mind that the important thing was to keep out intruders, especially at night.

At all events, this indispensable feature of the building's security has been complemented by others measures which ensure strict control of access.

In the first place, a metal railing set in the midst of bushes encircles the garden laid out around the building, from the top of the hill to its north and south boundaries, so that the area of the Pavilion is delimited by the railing, the wall of the Palau de Victòria Eugenia and the Pavilion itself.

In addition to this, visual control by means of closed-circuit television detects anyone approaching from the various points of access to the building. An underground alarm system is triggered by anyone approaching the building by way of the garden, while a network of beams controlled by photoelectric cells provides an invisible barrier protecting the front of the Pavilion.

Fig. 70. The structure of the podium and the concrete roof before being clad with stone.

Fig. 71. Platform and metal structures before being clad with stone.

Fig. 72. Detail of the metal structures supporting the travertine slabs.

Nevertheless, these various measures were not designed to definitively seal of a building whose *raison d'être* is circulation, openness and freedom of movement. Accordingly, the security measures we have introduced are no more than aids to the human surveillance of the security guards, who have ultimate control over everything taking place in and around the Pavilion.

Fig. 73. Positioning the windows in their stainless steel frames.

Some reflections on the services

The experience of carrying out the reconstruction posed numerous problems of detail, and in becoming aware of these we were led to reflect on various questions concerning the services, and the effectiveness or limitations of these. In conclusion, then, we would like to consider certain of these services: the drainage, the lighting and the heating.

These are all problems whose scope is very closely related to the permanence and diversity of use envisaged for the building in question. In the case of the building constructed in 1929, these were given specific local solutions rather than being incorporated into the overall design of the complex as a whole. Although we know that a new sewer was specially dug for the Pavilion, and a water supply provided, it is apparent that in general the complex problems of the drainage of the flat surfaces were approached in an extremely summary fashion. There are gradients indicated on the Köstner und Gottschalk working drawing which were probably not constructed. We also know that there was no guttering on the roofs and that the large pool had a small machine room with a pump, access to which was via the rear part of the wall looking towards the Palau de Victòria Eugenia.

As for the artificial lighting of the Pavilion, this was based on the idea of illumination through the box formed by the double sheet of etched glass which formed the light well, with electric light bulbs in the interior to reproduce the daylight which entered from above. The letters addressed to Mies van der Rohe by the people responsible for the maintenance of the building after its official opening make reference to the problems of increasing and improving the illumination, of training a spotlight on the Kolbe statue, and of the illumination of the surrounding area. These questions were left unresolved, evidently because of a lack both of time and of money in the budget. Limitations such as these give us a clearer understanding of the margins within which the project was conceived and executed, and within which formal inventiveness supplied its synthesizing and innovative response.

In our project the artificial lighting makes use of three types of solution. In the first instance, the reconstruction of the original system of nighttime illumination by means of a sandwich of white etched glass dividing the interior from the exterior. The electric bulbs which Mies used here have been replaced by two fluorescent strips, one for each sheet of glass, to give an almost uniform white light, diminishing slightly from floor to ceiling.

The second light source used in the interior spaces is provided by the inclusion of a series of sockets set into the floor to allow the installation of standard lamps which, particularly with halogen light reflected off the white plaster ceiling, offer a homogeneous illumination of the interior with no need for the addition of further extraneous elements on top of the clean sequence of planes which compose the space of the Pavilion. This simple solution was arrived at after consulting experts in lighting technology and assessing the projects they drew up, and in view of the insurmountable difficulties presented by any kind of solution using fixed spots or other light sources.

Finally, the scheme for the exterior combines soft illumination of the water in the pools with diffuse lighting around the building, amongst the trees and against the walls facing the building, guided at all times by the principle of making the building's form and volume recognizable rather than modifying it with beams of light which would undoubtedly conflict with the architectonic values of the building.

With regard to the heating, as in the case of the other services described above, we were confronted with the problems associated with the introduction of elements which would inevitably have a considerable impact on the final form of the building. The solutions we adopted are for this reason limited in scale. The roofed space of the Pavilion proper is provided with a single radiant heating system using electric radiators incorporated into the mass of the plaster rendering on the ceiling.

The administratrive offices are equipped with a complete air conditioning system, with the air circulation ducts installed inside the suspended floor and the air-conditioning machinery located in the service basement, a space added to the reconstruction project to accomodate the various services and storerooms the Pavilion requires.

We have not, however, included either of the two tables designed by Mies, which had tops of travertine to match the paving, and legs of the same type. Knoll International's experience proved to us that the large table which had stood by the white etched glass window was completely unstable, while the smaller table positioned by the onyx wall was almost as unsafe. Considering that an unsafe and uncertain attempt at reinstating these tables would be a poor compliment to the rest of Mies' incomparable furniture, we decided, at least initially, not to include these tables, production of which has long since been abandoned.

At the same time, Mies van der Rohe "took advantage" of the existing landscaping on the site, part of the gardens laid out by Forestier and Rubió i Tudurí when they set out to convert the hill of Montjuïc into a park in the middle of the second decade of the new century.

All of this induced us to recreate a comparable environment, above all bearing in mind the fact that many of the trees planted for the 1929 Exposition had survived in place. These somewhat abandoned plantations included umbras, magnolias, cypresses and laurels, a number of which were in a sufficiently precarious state as to need replacing, while others needed no more than a careful pruning to revitalize them.

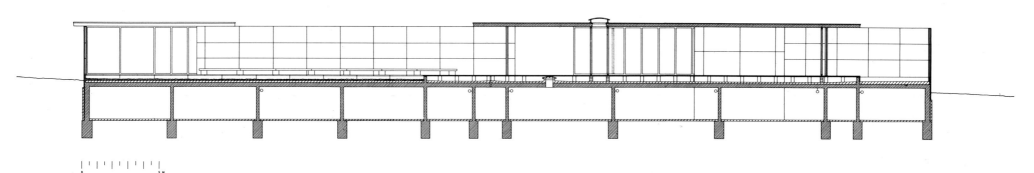

Fig. 74. Longitudinal section.

Furniture
The «Barcelona Chair» created by Mies van der Rohe for this building was clearly expected to occupy the place which Mies' project itself had set aside for it. Commercial exploitation and the subsequent copying of this famous design have not done justice to a type of chair whose refinement lies in the perfection of the finishing of both the metal and the leather elements.

The Knoll International company was able to supply us with versions of the chairs and the ottoman stools which are of the highest quality, in white kidskin, with a chromed metal frame precision soldered at the joints.

The administrative spaces are furnished with a combination of the M.R. chair, also manufactured by Knoll International, and standardized office furniture by Tecno.

Finally, the red curtain running in front of the transparent glas window is in double-sided velvet, and the black carpet is of machine-woven wool with a simple finish, also in black.

Landscaping
It is evident that Mies van der Rohe's intention here, as in other of his projects, was to create an effect of contrast between the strict geometry of the forms of his architecture and a natural backdrop of leafy green trees and shrubs.

Fig. 75. View of the exterior from the interior before putting in the translucent white glass.

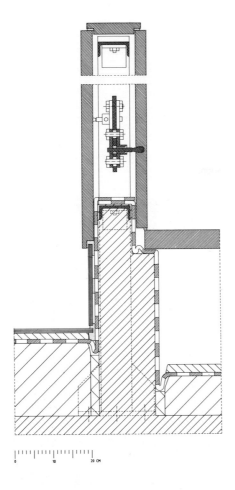

Fig. 77. Detail of the metalwork.

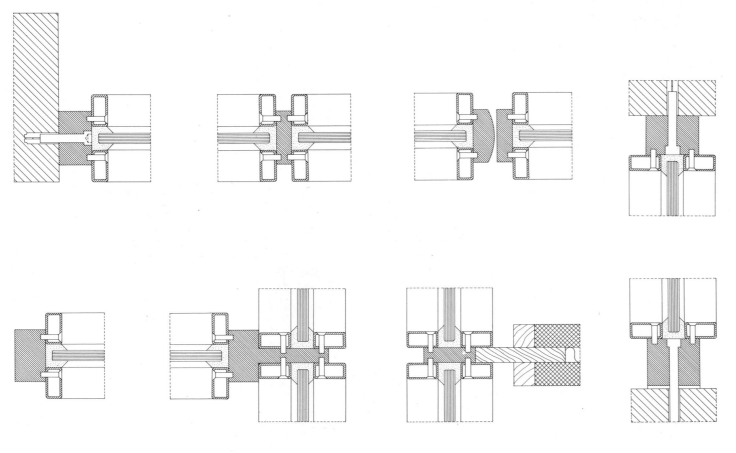

The ground around the Pavilion was treated in two ways, using coarse sand for the pedestrian access areas, and dark green Mediterranean ivy on the whole of the area to the rear. Masses of oleanders surrounded, as in the past, the administrative office building, while a row of umbras screened the metal railings ringing the perimeter of the protected area of the Pavilion.

The question of protocol concerning the flagpoles presented a slight problem, in that the indispensable pair of tall masts for the German and Spanish flags should by rights be complemented by a further three masts flying the flags of Spain, Catalonia and the city of Barcelona. This delicate matter of symbolism was resolved with the addition of a group of three somewhat shorter flagpoles set in front of the wall of the Palau de Victòria Eugènia, at the end of the perspective formed by the road running in front of the main facade of the Pavilion.

5. Final reflection: in defence of a replica

When Marcel Duchamp appended his signature and the words *pour copie, conforme* to the margin of the copy of the *Grand Verre* that Ulf Linde had produced for the Museum of Modern Art in Stockholm, he effectively ratified the end of the Romantic conception of the work of art. Duchamp himself had already carried out numerous operations in which all that remained to bridge the space between the object and its status as art was the deliberate intention on the part of the person who determined to undertake this significative act.

The *Grand Verre*, the *Glisière*, the *ready-mades*, were also reproduced on numerous occasions with Duchamp's explicit approval.

It is equally true that reproductions have served over the centuries to extend the repertoire of art. At his villa in Tivoli, Hadrian had imitations constructed of the architectures that most impressed him on his travels, in the same way that Lord Burlington was to recreate Palladian villas in the gardens at Chiswick, or the Venetians, in the early years of this century, rebuilt their *campanile* in front of the Cathedral of San Marco after it had fallen down.

And yet, despite these several illustrious precedents, we must in all honesty confess that we experienced a tremor of doubt when we had completed our reconstruction of the Pavilion erected by Mies van der Rohe in 1929 on the slopes of the hill of Montjuïc, in Barcelona.

This building, which we had seen reproduced dozens of times in all the major books on the history of art and architecture, whose simple plan we had studied on so many occasions without entirely grasping the distance between the clear order it seemed to reveal to us and the intellectual tension of the displaced elements, was an icon which for more than fifty years had been generating an intense energy, as a presence confined to the pages of books and magazines.

To reconstruct the Pavilion was, in these circumstances, a traumatic undertaking. On the one hand it meant entering into that Duchampesque perspective in which we had to accept, *hélas!*, a certain inanity in our aesthetic operations. It is hard to maintain the almost religious conviction that art is the reproduction of unique, unrepeatable and transcendent events when its reproductions fill the popular media, or when we are confronted by the conventional nature of its values.

Yet there was still a sense of daring in resolving to undertake the challenge of recreating, before our very eyes and in the three dimensions of physical space, what had for so long been essentially a graphic reference. To redraw the project that Mies van der Rohe had worked out under such great pressure late in 1928, to travel to the stone quarries of Italy, Greece and North Africa in search of similar materials, to make a hundred visits to the site selected by the architect, in order to construct there, in the reality of its dimensions, textures and colours, that image we all had in our minds, was, without a doubt, risky.

We have no doubt that all those of us who played some part in this undertaking are conscious of the distance that exists between the original and its replica. Not because the quality of its execution is inferior, which is not the case, or because it was impossible to determine precisely how all of the details of the building had been resolved, but because every replica is, indisputably, a *reinterpretation*.

In the same sense that it is impossible for us to hear the *St Matthew Passion* as Bach conducted it in the church of St Thomas in Leipzig, for all that we can enjoy brilliant and sensitive contemporary interpretations of it, so too for this masterpiece of modern architecture —"perhaps the most important building of this century", in Peter Behrens' words— what we have attempted to bring to a successful conclusion is an *interpretation*.

Faithful in the site of which it has been reconstructed, although at the moment suffering lamentably from the ugly presence of a bunker-like neighbouring building which is crying out for demolition; as exact as possible in the resolution of the details —"God himself is in the details", Mies himself remarked on more than one occasion—; painstaking in the choice of the materials and the dimensional layout, on which countless studies and consultations with technical specialists and experts on Mies' work were lavished; and finally, nevertheless, different, we know, this second version of that Pavilion that was constructed too hastily, with the excuse that it was only to last a few months, using the Third World technologies of 1929 Barcelona, leaving unresolved the conceptual problems which throughout his life Mies van der Rohe struggled again and again to work out in his buildings.

But the proof of all this, the most decisive proof, is something that cannot be explained by the printed pages of this book, except at the risk of falling, once again, inside the closed circle of paper architecture. It is necessary to go there, to walk amidst and see the startling contrast between the building and its surroundings, to let your gaze be drawn into the calligraphy of the patterned marble and its kaleidoscopic figures, to feel yourself enmeshed in a system of planes in stone, glass and water that envelops and moves you through space, and contemplate the hard, emphatic play of Kolbe's bronze dancer over the water. This is what we have tried to achieve and to offer to the sensibility and the culture of our time.

Fig. 78. Presentation of Kolbe's sculpture on its support.

Fig. 79. Positioning Kolbe's sculpture on its Alpine green marble pedestal.

0   5 CM

Fig. 80. Detail of the metal pillar.

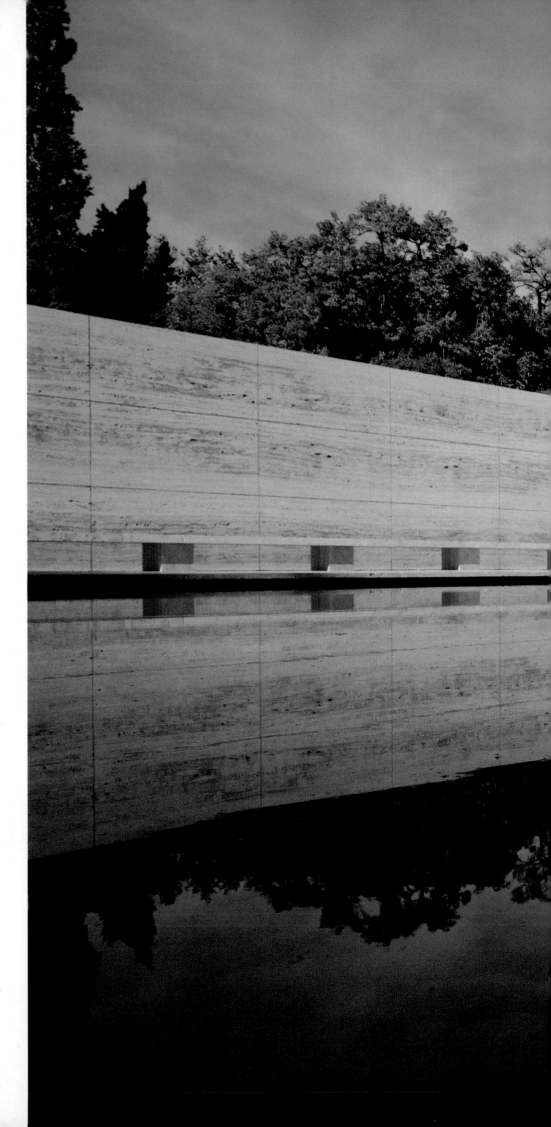

Fig. 83. The access stairway and the Pavilion.

Previous pages:
Fig. 81. Access stairway.

Fig. 82. The large pool and the Pavilion.   **Fig. 84.** The large pool and the Pavilion.

Fig. 87. The Pavilion from the service annexe area.

Fig. 85. The pedestal with the Pavilion.

Fig. 86. The large pool with the pedestal and the Pavilion.

Fig. 88. The platform by the large pool and the Pavilion.

Fig. 89. The bench and walls of travertine.

Fig. 90. The bench, the travertine wall and the stainless steel cruciform pillar.

Fig. 91. The service annexe pavilion and the travertine wall and bench.

Fig. 93. The pool with the travertine bench and walls.

Fig. 92. The service annexe pavilion from the rear entrance.

Fig. 96. The access stairway.

Fig. 94. The travertine wall and the pool.

Fig. 95. The Alpine green wall, the platform, the wall and the bench.

Fig. 97. The stainless steel metalwork and the service annexe pavilion.

Fig. 98. The travertine walls and the pool.

Fig. 99. The access stairway, the pedestal and the glass walls.

Fig. 100. The travertine wall and bench.

Fig. 101. The travertine wall and bench by the service annexe pavilion.

Fig. 102. The pool with the travertine wall and bench.

Fig. 104. Interior with the Barcelona couch.

Fig. 103. The stainless steel metalwork.

Fig. 105. Interior showing the effects of reflections and transparencies.

Fig. 106. Interior with the Barcelona chair and the cruciform pillar in the foreground.

Fig. 107. The onyx wall.

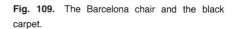
Fig. 108. The couch by the window of white glass.

Fig. 109. The Barcelona chair and the black carpet.

Fig. 110. The Barcelona chair and the onyx wall.

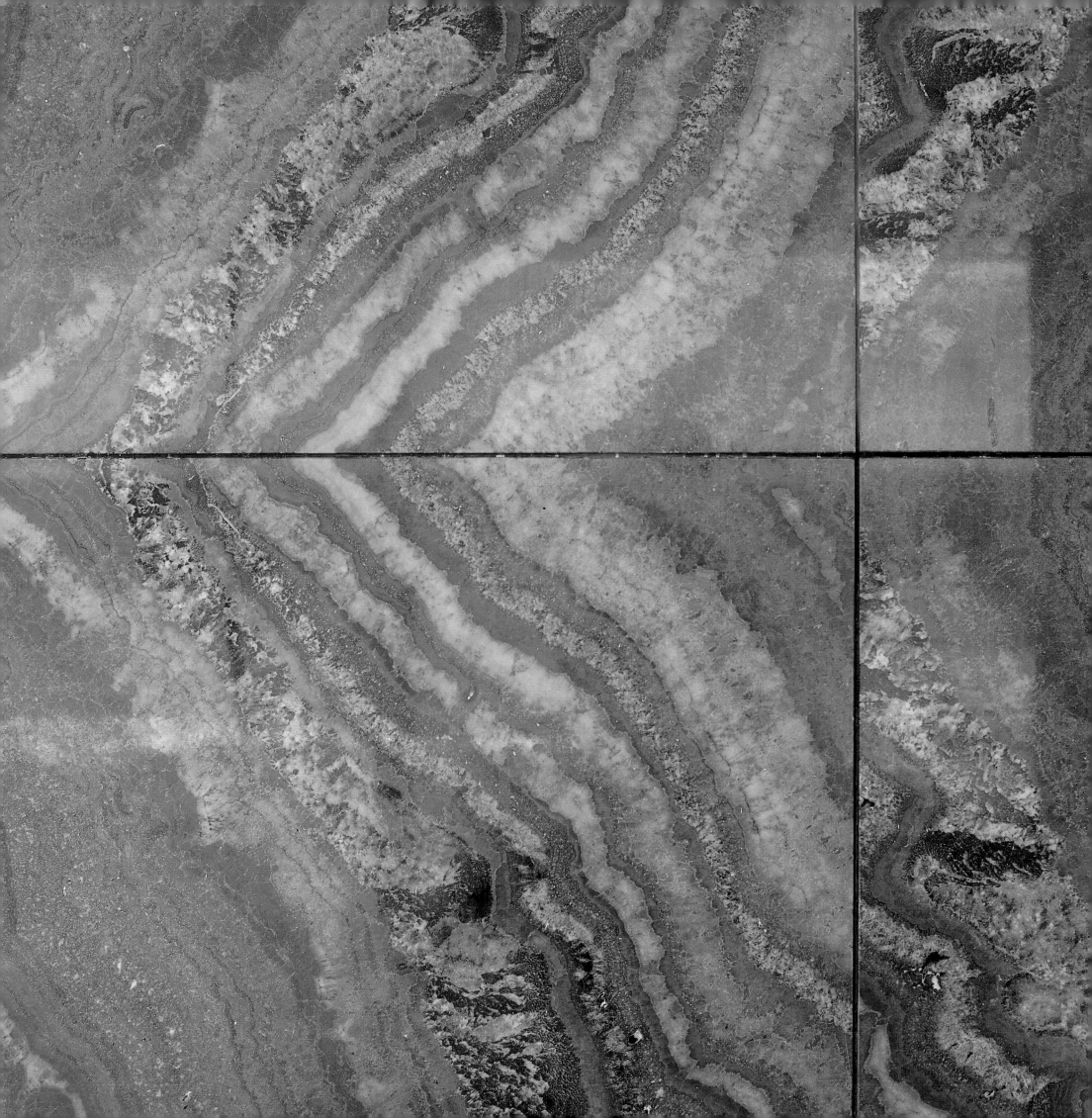

Fig. 112. The Barcelona chair.

Fig. 113. The Barcelona couch.

Fig. 111. The veining on the onyx wall.

Figs. 114 and 115. The sculpture by G. Kolbe.

Fig. 116. The sculpture by G. Kolbe seen from the Pavilion.

Fig. 117. The walls of travertine and Alpine green marble.

Fig. 118. The wall of Alpine green marble by the small pool.

Fig. 119. The small pool and the wall of Alpine green marble.

Fig. 120. The stainless steel cruciform pillar with the travertine base.

Fig. 123. The travertine with the roof.

Bibliography

1. Books

Argan, Giulio Carlo: *El arte moderno: 1770-1970*, 2 vols., Fernando Torres Editor, Valencia, 1975.

Banham, Reyner: *Teoría y diseño en la primera Era de la Máquina*, Ediciones Paidós Ibérica, S.A., Barcelona, 1985.

Benevolo, Leonardo: *Historia de la arquitectura moderna*, Editorial Gustavo Gili, S.A., Barcelona, 1987[6].

Benton, Tim: *El estilo internacional*, 2 vols., ADIR Editores, Madrid, 1981.

Bill, Max: *Mies van der Rohe*, Ediciones Infinito, Buenos Aires, 1956.

Blake, Peter: *Maestros de la arquitectura moderna: Le Corbusier, Mies van der Rohe, Frank Lloyd Wright*, Editorial Víctor Lerú, S.A., Buenos Aires, 1972.

Blaser, Werner: *Mies van der Rohe: el arte de la estructura* (trilingual edition), Carlos Hirsch Editor, Buenos Aires, 1965.

Blaser, Werner: *Mies van der Rohe*, Editorial Gustavo Gili, S.A., Barcelona, 1986[6].

Blaser, Werner: *Mies van der Rohe. Principles and School*, Zurich, 1977.

Blaser, Werner: *Mies van der Rohe. Furniture and Interiors*, London, 1982.

Bonta, Juan Pablo: *Anatomía de la interpretación en arquitectura. Reseña semiótica de la crítica del Pabellón de Barcelona de Mies van der Rohe*, Editorial Gustavo Gili, S.A., Barcelona, 1975.

Bonta, Juan Pablo: *Sistemas de significación en arquitectura. Un estudio de la arquitectura y su interpretación*, Editorial Gustavo Gili, S.A., Barcelona, 1977.

Calzà, Gianni/Giovanni Denti: *Mies van der Rohe. Il padiglione di Barcelona*, Alinea Editrice, Florence, 1989.

Carter, Peter: *Mies van der Rohe at Work*, London, 1974.

De Fusco, Renato: *Historia de la arquitectura contemporánea*, 2 vols., Hermann Blume Ediciones, Madrid, 1986[4].

Drexler, Arthur: *Ludwig Mies van der Rohe*, Editorial Bruguera, S.A., Barcelona, 1966[2].

Frampton, Kenneth: *Historia crítica de la arquitectura moderna*, Editorial Gustavo Gili, S.A., Barcelona, 1987[3].

Futagawa, Yukio/Ruyichi Hamaguchi/Meiji Watanabe: *Mies van der Rohe*, Tokyo, 1968.

Giedion, Siegfried: *Espacio, tiempo y arquitectura. El futuro de una nueva tradición*, Editorial Dossat, S.A., Madrid, 1980[5].

Glaeser, Ludwig: *Ludwig Mies van der Rohe. Drawings in the Collection of the Museum of Modern Art*, New York, 1969.

Glaeser, Ludwig: *Furniture and Furniture Drawings from the Design Collection at the Mies van der Rohe Archive*, New York, 1977.

Glaeser, Ludwig: *Ludwig Mies van der Rohe: The Barcellona Pavillion's 50th Anniversary*, Museum of Modern Art, New York, 1979.

Hilberseimer, Ludwig Karl: *Mies van der Rohe*, Chicago, 1953; Milan, 1984.

Hitchcock, Henry-Russell: *Modern Arquitecture*, New York, 1929; latest ed., 1970.

Hitchcock, Henry-Russell: *Arquitectura de los siglos XIX y XX,* Ediciones Cátedra, S.A., Madrid, 1981.

Hitchcock, Henry-Russell/Philip C. Johnson: *The International Style*, New York, 1932; latest ed., 1966.

H.S.: *Barcelona Weltausstellung 1929*, supplement with the newspaper *Erstes Morgenblatt*, Frankfurt am Main, 2, 5, 7 and 11 June, 1929.

Jencks, Charles R./George Baird (eds.): *El significado en arquitectura*, Hermann Blume Ediciones, Madrid, 1975.

Joedicke, Jürgen: *Arquitectura contemporánea. Evolución y tendencias*, Editorial Gustavo Gili, S.A., Barcelona, 1970.

Johnson, Philip C.: *Mies van der Rohe*, Editorial Víctor Lerú, S.A., Buenos Aires, 1961.

Johnson, Philip C.: *Escritos*, Introduction by Vincent Scully Jr., Prologue by Peter Eisenman and Commentaries by Robert A.M. Stern; Editorial Gustavo Gili, S.A., Barcelona, 1981.

Marsà, Àngel: *La montaña iluminada*, Barcelona, 1929.

Mies van der Rohe, Ludwig: *Escritos, diálogos y discursos*, Colegio Oficial de Aparejadores y Arquitectos de Murcia, Murcia, 1981.

Miller Cane, Barbara: *Architecture and Politics in Germany: 1918-1945*, Cambridge (Massachusetts), 1968.

Neumeyer, Fritz: *Mies van der Rohe, das Kunstlose Wort. Gedanken zur Baukunst*, Berlin, 1986.

Norberg-Schulz, Christian: *Casa Tugendhat House, Brno*, Rome, 1984.

Papi, Lorenzo: *Ludwig Mies van der Rohe*, Florence, 1975.

Pawley, Martin: *Mies van der Rohe*, London, 1970.

Pehnt, Wolfgang: *La arquitectura expresionista*, Editorial Gustavo Gili, S.A., Barcelona, 1975.

Pevsner, Nikolaus: *Iniciació a l'arquitectura*, Edicions 62, S.A., Barcelona, 1969 (Catalan edition); *Esquema de la arquitectura europea*, Ediciones Infinito, Buenos Aires, 1977.

Sanz Balza, Eliseo: *Notas de un Visitante. Exposición Internacional de Barcelona*, Barcelona, 1930 (collected articles: see Articles below).

Schulze, Franz: *Mies van der Rohe: Interior Spaces*, Chicago.

Schulze, Franz: *Mies van der Rohe. Una biografía crítica*, Hermann Blume Ediciones, Madrid, 1986 (in collaboration with the MOMA Archive).

Schulze, Franz: *Mies van der Rohe: Barcelona Pavillion and Furniture Design*, Knoll International, New York, 1986.

Schulze, Franz (ed.): *Mies van der Rohe. Critical Essays*, Museum of Modern Art/Mit Press, Cambridge (Massachusetts), 1989.

Scully Jr., Vincent: *L'Architecture Moderne*, New York, 1961; Paris, 1962.

Sharp, Dennis: *Historia en imágenes de la arquitectura del siglo XX*, Editorial Gustavo Gili, S.A., Barcelona, 1973.

Sharp, Dennis: *The Rationalists,* London, 1978.

Solà-Morales, Ignasi de: *Eclecticismo y vanguardia. El caso de la Arquitectura Moderna en Catalunya*, Editorial Gustavo Gili, S.A., Barcelona, 1980.

Solà-Morales, Ignasi de: *L'Exposició Internacional de Barcelona 1914-1929. Arquitectura i Ciutat*, Barcelona, 1985.

Spaeth, David A.: *Ludwig Mies van der Rohe: An Annotated Bibliography and Chronology*, New York, 1979.

Spaeth, David A.: *Mies van der Rohe*, Preface by Kenneth Frampton; Editorial Gustavo Gili, S.A., Barcelona, 1986.

Tafuri, Manfredo/Francesco Dal Co: *Arquitectura contemporánea*, Aguilar, S.A. de Ediciones, Madrid, 1978.

Tafuri, Manfredo: *La esfera y el laberinto. Vanguardias y arquitectura de Piranesi a los años setenta*, Editorial Gustavo Gili, S.A., Barcelona, 1984.

Tedeschi, Enrico: *Teoría de la arquitectura*, Ediciones Nueva Visión, S.A.I.C., Buenos Aires, 1962.

Tegethoff, Wolf: *Mies van der Rohe. Die Villen und Landhausprojekte*, Essen, 1981.

Various authors: *Exposición Internacional de Barcelona 1929. Catálogo oficial*, Barcelona, 1929.

Various authors: *Internationale Ausstellung. Deutsche Abteilung* (catalogue in German), Barcelona, 1929.

Various authors: *Barcelona 1929-1930. Recuerdo de la Exposición. Anuario de la Ciudad*, Publicación Oficial de la Sociedad de Atracción de Forasteros (Syndicat d'Initiative), Barcelona, 1930.

Various authors: *Las exposiciones de Barcelona Universal de 1988 e Internacional de 1929*, Freixenet, Barcelona, 1939.

Various authors: *Mies van der Rohe*, London, 1986.

Various authors: *El Pavelló Alemany de Mies van der Rohe 1929-1986*, Ajuntament de Barcelona, Barcelona, 1987.

Werner, Bruno E.: *Die Neue Architektur in Deutschland*, Academy Editions/St. Martin's Press, Munich, 1952.

Zevi, Bruno: *Architettura in Nuce. Una definición de arquitectura*, Aguilar, S.A. de Ediciones, Madrid, 1969.

Zevi, Bruno: *Saber ver la arquitectura. Ensayo sobre la interpretación espacial de la arquitectura*, Editorial Poseidón, S.L., Barcelona, 1978[2].

Zevi, Bruno: *Historia de la arquitectura moderna*, Editorial Poseidón, S.L., Barcelona, 1980.

2. Articles

2a. *Signed articles*

Ajuntament de Barcelona: «Aprovar la menció de la Fundació Pública Municipal del Pavelló Alemany ''Mies van der Rohe''», in *Gaseta Municipal de Barcelona*, year LXX, n.º 14, May 20, 1983.

A.M.: «Barcelona recupera l'edifici de Mies van der Rohe», in *Avui*, Tuesday, October 11, 1983.

Bakema, Jakob Berend: «Nota sobre Mies», in *Bauen + Wohnen*, n.º 5, May 1968.

Bassegoda Nonell, Juan: «Historia y anécdota de una obra de Mies van der Rohe», in *La Vanguardia*, October 6, 1979.

Bernoulli, Hans: «Der Pavillon des Deutschen Reiches und Internationalen Austellung, Barcelona 1929», in *Werk*, n.º 11, November 1929, pp. 350-351.

Bloc, André: «Mies van der Rohe», in *L'Architecture d'Aujourd'hui*, n.º 113-114, April-May 1984.

Bohigas, Oriol: «La obra barcelonesa de Mies van der Rohe», in *Cuadernos de Arquitectura*, n.º 21, March 1955.

Bohigas, Oriol: «A los 25 años. La obra maestra de la Exposición del 29», in *Destino*, October 9, 1954.

Boix, José: «Mies van der Rohe 1886-1969», in *Cúpula*, n.º 242, December 1969, pp. 726-730.

Borràs, Jordi: «Barcelona volverá a tener el pabellón más importante de la Exposición de 1929», in *La Vanguardia*, Tuesday October 11, 1983.

Calzina, P.: «Les arts decoratives a Montjuïc», in *D'Ací i d'Allà*, special «Exposició Internacional de Barcelona», issue, December 1929, pp. 80-83.

Carbonell, J.: «El Pavelló Alemany de l'Exposició de 1929», in *Butlletí-Revista de l'Associació del Personal de la Caixa de Pensions*, n.º 162, October 1984.

Carol, Màrius: «El Ayuntamiento proyecta reconstruir un pabellón racionalista de la Feria de 1929», in *El País*, Friday, February 18, 1983.

Carter, Peter: «Mies van der Rohe - The Barcelona Pavilion», in *AD*, March 1961, pp. 100-101.

Carter, Peter: «Los espacios urbanos de Mies», in *Cuadernos Summa - Nueva Visión*, n.º 42, December 1969.

Ciammitti, Mario/Giuseppe Di Giovine: «Per conoscere il Padiglione di Mies», in *Parametro*, n.º 122, December 1983.

Cirici, Cristian/Fernando Ramos/Ignasi de Solà-Morales: «La reconstrucción del Pabellón de Mies van der Rohe», in *El País*, Sunday, May 29, 1983.

Cirici, Cristian/Fernando Ramos/Ignasi de Solà-Morales: «Proyecto de reconstrucción del Pabellón Alemán de la Exposición Internacional de Barcelona 1929», in *Arquitecturas bis*, n.º 44, july 1983, pp. 6-17.

Cirici, Cristian/Fernando Ramos/Ignasi de Solà-Morales: «Proyecto de reconstrucción del Pabellón de Mies van der Rohe», in *El Croquis*, n.º 9-10, 1983, pp. 59-63.

Cirici, Cristian/Fernando Ramos/Ignasi de Solà-Morales: «Davant la reconstrucció del Pavelló Alemany de l'Exposició de 1929», in *Serra d'Or*, n.º 312, September 1985.

Dearstyne, Howard: «Miesian Space Concept in Domestic Architecture», in *A + V*, n.º 103, April 1979, pp. 3-8.

Dorner, Alexander/Franz Roh/Hildebrand Gurlitt: «Was sollen jetzt ausstellungen?», «Ausstellungen von heute» and «Museen und ausstellungen in...», in *Das Neue Frankfurt*, June 1930, pp. 143-147.

Evans, Robin: «Mies van der Rohe's paradoxical symmetries», in *A A Files*, n.º 19, Spring 1990.

Fortuny, Epifanio de: «Alemania en el Palacio de Agricultura», in *Exposición Internacional de Barcelona. Diario Oficial*, n.º 34, October 26, 1929.

Frampton, Kenneth: «Modern Architecture 1920-1945», in *G.A. Document*, n.º 3, special issue, January 1983.

Francklyn Paris, William: «The Barcelona Exposition. A Splendid but Costly Effort of the Catalan People», in *The Architectural Forum*, n.º 5, October 1929, pp. 481-495.

Fullaondo, Juan Daniel: «Humanismo y paradoja en la obra de Mies van der Rohe», in *Nueva Forma*, n.º 9, October 1966.

Galceran, Anna: Mies van der Rohe', in *El País*, Tuesday, October 11, 1983.

García Roa, Isidro: in *Exposición Internacional de Barcelona. Diario Oficial*, n.º 34, October 26, 1929.

Garrut, Josep Maria: «La arquitectura de la Exposición Internacional de Barcelona de 1929», in *Diario de Barcelona*, September 3, 1969.

Genzmer, Walter: «Die Internationale Ausstellung in Barcelona», in *Zentralblatt der Bauverwaltung*, n.º 34, August 21, 1929, pp. 541-545.

Genzmer, Walter: «Der Deutsche Reichspavillon auf der Internationalen Ausstellung Barcelona», in *Die Baugilde*, n.º 1, 1929, pp. 1654-1657.

Gifreda, Màrius: «L'arquitectura de l'Exposició», in *D'Allí i d'Allà*, special issue «Exposició Internacional de Barcelona», December 1929, pp. 89-93.

Giralt-Miracle, Daniel: «Mies van der Rohe (1886-1969)», in *Goya*, n.º 93, November-December de 1969.

Harbers, Guido: «Deutscher Reichspavillon in Barcelona auf der Internationalen Ausstellung 1929», in *Der Baumeister*, n.º 27, 1929, pp. 421-427.

Hays, K. Michael: «The Critical Architecture of Mies van der Rohe», in *Perspecta*, n.º 21, 1984.

Honey, Sandra: «Who and What Inspired Mies van der Rohe in Germany», in *Architectural Design*, n.º 3-4, 1979, pp. 99-102.

Honey, Sandra: «The Office of Mies van der Rohe in America. The Towers», in *International Architect*, n.º 3, 1983, pp. 43-54.

Kühne, Günther: «La forma pura», in *Cuadernos Summa - Nueva Visión*, n.º 42, December 1969.

Kuh, Katharine: «Mies van der Rohe. Une interview et un portrait», in *Informations et Documents*, n.º 227, May 1966, pp. 20-23.

Lope Vélez, Fray: «La escultura alemana y los tópicos de la post-guerra», in *Exposición Internacional de Barcelona. Diario Oficial*, n.º 44, January 4, 1930.

Loyer, François: «Mies, l'homme d'une idée», in *L'Oeil*, n.º 191, November 1970, pp. 18-23.

Mackay, David: «De la Revolució espartaquista al Pavelló de Barcelona», in *Serra d'Or*, October 1968; *Nueva Forma*, n.º 86, March 1973.

Malcolmson, Reginald M.: «La obra de Mies van der Rohe», in *Hogar y Arquitectura*, n.º 108-109, monograph issue, 1973.

Martí Arís, Carles: «Mies es más», in *El Noticiero Universal*, Tuesday, March 17, 1981.

McGrath, Raymond: «Looking into Glass», in *Architectural Review*, January 1932, pp. 29-30.

Melis, Paolo: «Questa è una casa», in *Domus*, n.º 633, November 1982.

Montaner, Josep Maria: «La arquitecta Smithson duda de la conveniencia de reconstruir el Pabellón Mies van der Rohe», in *El País*, November 15, 1985.

Nicolini, Renato: «Mies, l'epilogo», in *Controspazio*, n.º 4-5, April-May 1970, pp. 92-95.

Norton, Paul F.: «World's Fairs into the 1930s», in *Journal of the Society of Architectural Historians*, n.º 1, March 1965, pp. 27-30.

Ogden Hannaford, R.: «Missing Mies», in *Architectural Record*, July 1979, pp. 97 y 110.

Padovan, Richard: «Mies van der Rohe Reinterpreted», in *UIA*, n.º 3, 1983, pp. 39-42.

Paul, Jacques: «German Neo-classicism and the Modern Movement», in *Architectural Review*, n.º 907, September 1972.

Persico, Edoardo: «L'architetto Mies van der Rohe», in *Casabella*, n.º 7, 1931.

Quetglas, Josep: «Pérdida de la síntesis: El Pabellón de Mies», in *Carrer de la Ciutat*, n.º 11, April 1980, pp. 17-27.

Quetglas, Josep: «El Pavelló de Mies», in *Grans temes «L'Avenç»*, n.º 3, 1979, pp. 59-68.

Ramírez de Lucas, Juan: «Los ochenta años de Mies van der Rohe», in *Arquitectura*, n.º 91, July 1966, pp. 52-57.

Ramos, Fernando: «El Pabellón de Barcelona y la influencia de Mies van der Rohe», in *El Noticiero Universal*, Tuesday, March 17, 1981.

Ravetllat, Pere-Joan: «Primer van ser les parets...», in *Quaderns d'Arquitectura i Urbanisme*, n.º 163, 1985.

Rendal, Will: «Mies Revival», in *The Architect's Journal*, n.º 18, vol. 183, April 30, 1986, pp. 40-46.

Rgbg., Frida: «Barcelona vista por un alemán», in *Exposición Internacional de Barcelona. Diario Oficial*, n.º 35, November 2, 1929.

Ricart, Marta: «El Pabellón de Mies van der Rohe de Montjuïc será utilizado como sede de actos culturales», in *La Vanguardia*, December 29, 1985, p. 20.

Romaní, Marta: «Sillas siglo XX», in *Exposición Internacional de Barcelona. Diario Oficial*, n.° 35, November 2, 1929.

Rubió Tudurí, Nicolau Maria: «Le Pavillon de l'Allemagne à l'Exposition de Barcelone», in *Cahiers d'Art*, vol. 4, 1929, pp. 408-411; *Carrer de la Ciutat*, n.° 11, April 1980, p. 16.

Sáenz de Valicourt, A.: «Mies van der Rohe y su obra magistral», in *Técnica de la Construcción*, n.° 18, November 1983, pp. 72-75.

Sala i Duch, Francesc: «El Pavelló Mies van der Rohe no es pot deixar perdre», in *Serra d'Ort*, year IX, n.° 4, April 1967, pp. 11-12.

Sanz Balza, Eliseo: «Notas de un visitante. Avenidas - Paseos - Plazas - Palacios - Pabellones», in *Exposición Internacional de Barcelona. Diario Oficial*, n.° 46, January 18, 1930.

Sanz Balza, Eliseo: «Notas de un visitante. Juegos de agua - Iluminaciones», in *Exposición Internacional de Barcelona. Diario Oficial*, n.° 50, February 15, 1930.

Sanz Balza, Eliseo: «Notas de un visitante. Palacios de la Avenida de María Cristina y Plaza del Universo», in *Exposición Internacional de Barcelona. Diario Oficial*, n.°, 53, march 8, 1930.

Sanz Balza, Eliseo: «Notas de un visitante. (continuation)», in *Exposición Internacional de Barcelona. Diario Oficial*, n.° 54, March 15, 1930.

Sanz Balza, Eliseo: «Notas de un visitante. Palacios y pabellones del Grupo de Santa Madrona», in *Exposición Internacional de Barcelona. Diario Oficial*, n.° 55, March 22, 1930.

Sanz Balza, Eliseo: «Notas de un visitante. Palacios y pabellones Sección Internacional», in *Exposición Internacional de Barcelona. Diario Oficial*, n.° 56, March 29, 1930.

Schulze, Franz: «The Barcelona Pavillon Returns», in *Arts in America*, vol. 67, n.° 7, November 1979, pp. 98-103.

Sepliarsky, Elina Sara: «I segni e le "Figure" del Padiglione di Barcellona», in *Op. cit.*, n.° 32, January 1975, pp. 68-75.

Serenyi, Peter: «Mies' New National Gallery: An Essay on Architectural Content», in *The Harvard Architectural Review*, vol. 1, Spring 1980, pp. 180-189.

Serrano Freixas, Ángel: «El ámbito cultural de Mies van der Rohe», in *Cuadernos de Arquitectura*, n.° 70, 1967.

Smithson, Alison: «La sensació del lloc en el Pavelló», in *Quaderns d'Arquitectura i Urbanisme*, n.° 163, 1984.

Smithson, Peter: «Retorn. Mies revisitat», in *Quaderns d'Arquitectura i Urbanisme*, n.° 163, 1984.

Solà-Morales i Rubió, Ignasi de: «L'arquitectura de l'Exposició. Palaus i pavellons», in *Grans Temes «L'Avenç»*, n.° 3, April 1979, pp. 3-17.

Solà-Morales i Rubió, Ignasi de: «La Exposición Internacional de Barcelona: Arquitecturas contaminadas», in *CAU*, n.° 57, 1979.

Solà-Morales i Rubió, Ignasi de: «Arquitectures per a Gran Barcelona: L'Exposició Universal 1914-1929», ei *L'Avenç*, n.° 24, February 1980, pp. 55-60.

Solà-Morales i Rubió, Ignasi de: «Reconstrucción del Pabellón Mies van der Rohe», in *La Vanguardia*, Tuesday, May 3, 1983.

Solé de Sojo, Vicenç: «Montjuich Block-Notas», in *Barcelona Atracción*, November 1929, p. 350.

Spiegel, Olga: «Barcelona celebrará el centenario del nacimiento de Mies van der Rohe inaugurando su Pabellón», in *La Vanguardia*, September 14, 1985.

Suárez, Alícia/Mercè Vidal: «L'Exposició del 29», in *Serra d'Or*, year XXII, n.° 246, March 1980, pp. 57-59.

Takayama, Masami: «Mies van der Rohe», in *A + U*, n.° 124, January 1981.

Tegethoff, Wolf: «On the Development of the Conception of Space in the Works of Mies van der Rohe», in *Daidalos*, n.° 13, September 1984.

Tharrats, Joan-Josep: «Artistas de hoy: Mies van der Rohe», in *Revista de actualidades, artes y letras*, April 25-May 2, 1958.

Tihms, Fritz: «Architektur und Plastik», in *Die Baugilde*, n.° 12, January 1930, pp. 806-809.

Trebbi, Giorgio: «Mies a Barcellona. Mies a Bologna», in *Parametro*, n.° 121, November 1983.

Ulsamer, Federico: «Bienvenida al Pabellón Mies van der Rohe», in *Cúpula*, n.° 242, Decembere 1969, pp. 742-748.

Vayreda, Raimon: «Els moderns seients metàl·lics», in *D'Ací i d'Allà*, n.° 151, vol. XIX, July 1930, pp. 226-227.

Warre, James: «Barcelona» in *Progressive Architecture*, August 1986.

Zevi, Bruno: «Mies van der Rohe e Frank Lloyd Wright, poeti dello spazio», in *Metron*, n.° 37, 1950.

Zevi, Bruno: «Mies il Magnifico», *L'Espresso*, September 28, 1986.

2b. *Unsigned articles (in order of publication)*

«La concurrencia extranjera», in *Barcelona Atracción*, May 1929, pp. 131-134.

«La aportación extranjera a la Exposición de Barcelona», in *Exposición Internacional de Barcelona. Diario Oficial*, n.° 3, May 5, 1929, p. 27.

«La Sección Alemana de la Exposición Internacional de Barcelona 1929», in *Exposición Internacional de Barcelona. Diario Oficial*, n.° 10, May 25, 1929, p. 18.

«Alemania en la Exposición de Barcelona», in *Exposición Internacional de Barcelona. Diario Oficial*, n.° 11, May 26, 1929.

«Inauguración de la Secció d'Alemanya», in *La Nau*, May 27, 1929, p. 7.

«Sus Majestades han inaugurado esta mañana las secciones de Alemania y Finlandia», in *El Noticiero Universal*, May 27, 1929, p. 6.

«Esta mañana se han inaugurado las secciones de Alemania y Finlandia, asistiendo SS.MM.», in *La Noche*, May 27, 1929, p. 22.

«Inauguración de la Sección Alemana», in *Las Noticias*, May 28, 1929, p. 8.

«Inauguración del Pabellón de Alemania», in *Diario de Barcelona*, May 28, 1929.

Nota de Redacción, in *El Matí*, May 28, 1929, p. 5.

«Inauguración de secciones. La de Alemania», in *El Día Gráfico*, May 28, 1929.

«Inauguración del Pabellón de Alemania», in *La Vanguardia*, Tueday, May 28, 1929, p. 11.

«Inauguración de la Sección Alemana», in *El Correo Catalán*, May 28, de 1929.

«La Sección Alemana», in *El Diluvio*, Tuesday, May 28, 1929, p. 12.

«Notas de la Exposición», in *La Aurora*, Tuesday, May 28, 1929, p. 5.

«La inauguració del Pavelló d'Alemanya», in *La Publicitat*, Tuesday, May 28, 1929, p. 4.

«Una visita al Pavelló i a les dependències alemanyes», in *La Nau*, May 28, 1929, p. 6.

«Visita a la Secció d'Alemanya», in *La Veu de Catalunya*, May 29, 1929.

«Inauguración del Pabellón de Alemania», in *Barcelona ante la Exposición*, year II, n.° 11, June, 1929.

«Inauguración del Pabellón y Sección Alemana. El acto oficial», in *Exposición Internacional de Barcelona. Diario Oficial*, n.° 12, June 2, 1929, p. 14.

«Una visita a la Sección Alemana de la Exposición de Barcelona», in *Exposición Internacional de Barcelona. Diario Oficial*, n.° 12, June 2, 1929, p. 30.

«La actividad de la industria eléctrica alemana...», in *Exposición Internacional de Barcelona. Diario Oficial*, n.° 12, June 2, 1929, p. 25.

«La participación de Alemania en nuestro Certamen», in *Exposición Internacional de Barcelona. Diario Oficial*, n.° 13, June 9, 1929, p. 11.

«La Sección Alemana de Artes Gráficas», in *Exposición Internacional de Barcelona. Diario Oficial*, n.° 13, June 9, 1929, p. 12.

«La participación de Alemania», in *Gaceta de la Industria y del Comercio*, August 1929.

«Inauguración de los pabellones extranjeros», in *Barcelona Atracción*, August 1929, pp. 239-246.

«Programa de la Semana Alemana», in *Exposición Internacional de Barcelona. Diario Oficial*, n.° 33, October 19, 1929.

«La Semana Alemana», in *El Liberal*, October 19, 1929, p. 1.

«Semana Alemana», in *Diario de Barcelona*, October 20, 1929.

«La Sección Alemana. El acto inaugural», in *Las Noticias*, October 20, 1929.

«Semana Alemana», in *Diario de Barcelona*, October 23, 1929.

«Semana Alemana», in *Diario de Barcelona*, October 24, 1929.

«Semana Alemana», in *Diario de Barcelona*, October 25, 1929.

«Semana Alemana», in *Diario de Barcelona*, October 26, 1929.

«La aportación de Alemania a la Exposición de Barcelona», in *Exposición Internacional de Barcelona. Diario Oficial*, n.° 34, October 26, 1929.

«Libros alemanes sobre España», in *Exposición Internacional de Barcelona. Diario Oficial*, n.º 34, October 26, 1929.

«Alemania en el Palacio del Arte Textil», in *Exposición Internacional de Barcelona. Diario Oficial*, n.º 34, October 26, 1929.

«Fiestas y Congresos», in *Barcelona Atracción*, December 1929, pp. 367-375.

«La Exposición y sus maravillas vistas en avión», in *La Ilustración Iberoamericana*, vol. I, n.º 1, December 1929.

«Recorrent l'Exposició», in *Catalònia*, year IV, n.º 23, January 1930.

«El mobiliari a l'Exposició I», in *Mirador*, año II, n.º 61, jueves 27 de marzo de 1930, p. 7.

«Alemania», in *La Ilustración Iberoamericana*, April 1930.

«Debut Works of Architects: Mies van der Rohe - German Pavilion», in *The Kokusai-Kentiku*, n.º 10, October 1966.

«Nota sobre el Pabellón», in *Revista Nacional de Arquitectura*, n.º 183, March 1957.

«La arquitectura en la Exposición Internacional de Barcelona», in *Diario de Barcelona*, September 3, 1969, p. 14.

«Zum Tode von Ludwig Mies van der Rohe 1886-1969», in *Werk*, n.º 10, October 1969.

«El Pabellón de Mies van der Rohe», in *La Vanguardia*, January 29, 1970.

«El Pabellón de Mies van der Rohe», in *La Vanguardia*, May 17, 1970.

«Se pide la reconstrucción del ''Pabellón Barcelona''», in *La Vanguardia*, September 27, 1979.

«Les 50 ans du Pavillon de Barcelone», in *L'Architecture d'Aujourd'hui*, n.º 207, February 1980.

«Le Pavillon de Barcelone», in *Connaissance*, n.º 33, November 1979, pp. 94-95.

«El Pabellón de Mies van der Rohe se reconstruirá el próximo año», in *La Vanguardia*, March 16, 1983.

«Expuesta en el Born la maqueta del Pabellón de 1929 que reconstruirá el Ayuntamiento», in *El País*, Monday, May 7, 1983.

«La reconstrucción del Pabellón de Mies van der Rohe se iniciará en diciembre», in *La Vanguardia*, November 17, 1984.

«Alison Smithson abre hoy el curso en la Escuela de Arquitectura», in *La Vanguardia*, November 15, 1985.

Photographic credits

Arxiu Càtedra Composició ETSAB, Barcelona
nos 2 and 42
Arxiu Fundació Mies van der Rohe, Barcelona
nos 51 and 52
Arxiu Toni Castany, Barcelona
nos 41
Arxiu Vic Carrera, "Carrer de la Ciutat"
nos 33
Deutsche Bauzeitung
nos 31
Eloi Bonjoch, Barcelona
nos 81, 82, 83, 84, 85, 86, 87, 88, 89, 90, 91, 92, 93, 94, 95, 96, 97, 98, 99, 100,
101, 102, 103, 104, 105, 106, 107, 108, 109, 110, 111, 112, 113, 114, 115, 116, 117,
118, 119, 120, 121, 122 and 123
Fernando Ramos, Barcelona
nos 58, 59, 60, 61, 65, 66, 67, 68, 71, 72, 73, 75, 78 and 79
Hendrich Blessing Photographers
nos 47
Institut Municipal d'Historia, Barcelona
nos 1, 3, 32, 39, 46 and 48
Lluís Casals, Barcelona
nos 64 and 70
Mies van der Rohe Archive, The Museum of Modern Art, MOMA, New York
nos 7, 8, 9, 10, 11, 12, 13, 14, 15, 16, 17, 18, 19, 20, 21, 22, 24, 26, 27, 28, 29, 30,
34, 35, 36, 37, 38, 40, 43, 44, and 45
Staatliche Museen, Preussischer Kulturbesitz, Kunstbibliothek, Berlin
nos 4, 5 and 6